Living With Depression

written by Paul Hill
edited by Darin Jewell

authorHOUSE™

1663 LIBERTY DRIVE, SUITE 200
BLOOMINGTON, INDIANA 47403
(800) 839-8640
WWW.AUTHORHOUSE.COM

First published by AuthorHouse 08/01/05

ISBN: 1-4208-5924-2 (sc)

Printed in the United States of America
Bloomington, Indiana

This book is printed on acid-free paper.

Table of Contents

CHAPTER 1   WHEN I WAS A LAD   1

CHAPTER 2   A FAMILY THING   14

CHAPTER 3   HOLIDAYS   31

CHAPTER 4   SCHOOL DAYS   44

CHAPTER 5   COLLEGE AND BEYOND   68

CHAPTER 6   LIFE AT THE BAY   88

CHAPTER 7   BODELWYDDAN CASTLE   106

CHAPTER 8   RELATIONSHIPS   128

CHAPTER 9   HOME AGAIN   147

CHAPTER 10 UNIVERSITY   162

CHAPTER 11 RETURN FROM UNIVERSITY   182

CHAPTER 12 SUICIDAL THOUGHTS   199

CHAPTER 13 TALKING TO SHRINKS   215

CHAPTER 14 HOPES, DREAMS AND
                     ASPIRATIONS   232

CHAPTER ONE
WHEN I WAS A LAD

I was born in 1973 on January the 16th. I sometimes wonder if it was grey, overcast, murky day, in keeping with my life. My family lived in an area of Nottingham called Sneinton Dale - a working class area, not twenty minutes by foot from the city. My dad was just starting a career as an electrician and my mother had to look after two hungry, noisy, young kids.

My mother told me when they first moved into the house in Sneinton, my parents didn't have the money to buy their own furniture. They had to borrow and make do - just the same as the rest of the people who lived in the 'dale'. That's why my dad had to work away from home. It was something he regrets doing because he didn't get to see the family enough or watch is children grow up. My dad got used to being away from home. So did we. In the eighties, he spent 16 months working in the Falkland Islands at Port Stanley Airport.

When I was about two and my elder sister was four, we moved to Carlton, where my parents still live today. Carlton is slightly more 'upper-class' than Sneinton. It's a soft area. Nothing ever happens there. No robbery and no fighting.

The atmosphere and environment are leisurely and casual. Carlton is only about a thirty-minute walk from Sneinton - but it's uphill all the way! Carlton is surrounded by hills. You cannot go anywhere without having to do battle with a hill, and there's usually only one winner!

I suppose, looking back, I was lucky that we moved into that area. On the road that our house was located were a lot of young families of similar age to ours. A lot of what I remember as a young boy growing up is painful, but there are also great bursts of sunshine and light. I was part of a pretty unremarkable gang between the ages of nine and twelve years of age.

The worst part of my life, at that time, was the bed-wetting problem. It was more than a problem - it was horrendous. The thesaurus defines the term with such words as, dreadful and unbearable. I could have used either of those. All three of them in fact.

This period of my life had major repercussions on my life later on - it influenced the way I thought and more importantly, what I thought of myself. The real struggle that a depressed person has is not with the world or outside influences. The real conflict and the real bloodletting lies behind the false smile. The real fight comes maintaining a façade - a false smile here, a false laugh there. Anything to look like you're fitting in. And all the time, there's a tornado causing havoc inside, where it really counts.

I put my mum and dad through hell and for this I'm truly sorry. I cannot convey my love, respect and admiration enough for them. However, years on, I recall having a pretty emotional conversation with my dad, and him telling me that he didn't know how else to handle the situation. He told me there's no manual or handbook on how to bring up children. My dad's approach was a tough one. He believed that the way to solve the mystery of my bed-wetting, which lasted until I was fourteen, was by punishment. I am living testimony to the fact the punishment wasn't the answer.

The deal was that if I wet the bed, I would bring down the sheets and pyjamas and simply put them in the washing machine, apologise for what I'd done and then go about the normal business of doing last minute homework or panicking about something before I left for school. If only. If only life were that simple!

I went to extraordinary lengths of keep the floods at bay, or to 'build a dam for the night'. I cannot properly put the feelings down in words. I tried a method of placing both hands around my genitals, so if the damn burst, I'd be awoken straight away and be able to react with lightening speed! It didn't work. My next earth-shattering plan was to wait for it, stay up all night! That didn't work either. I was desperate.

While this was going on, I was still living an 'ordinary' little boy's life. My dad was punishing me now on a regular basis, and I quickly learned that the goalposts were moving. The deal was that I would bring down the wet 'stuff,' and my part would be done. It never turned out that way. I can't remember how it started, but I think I made a deal with my dad that if I hid the 'stuff' or didn't tell my parents, then I was in line for a 'good hiding', as my dad used to say.

The punishment included being given a cold shower. The cold water drumming on my head was painful. It was a horrible. It was even more frustrating when I hadn't broke my end of the deal! My dad was growing more and more frustrated. He told me I was costing him a fortune in washing powder! I think, in truth, he was angry and frustrated at having his son, his only son, blighted by wetting the bed. As I grew older, his feelings of disappointment in me would become like an irritating itch.

My mum had her part to play too. What did she do while all this was going on? Nothing really. My dad is

3

a completely different person now. That's one of those sayings that's tossed around with a weight of a plastic bag. People don't change - society changes around them and they stay the same, giving off an impression to the outside world that the person has changed. But in the case of my dad, and to a lesser, but no less significant sense my mum, they did both change.

My dad was aggressive at this time and my mum was, well, a wallflower, subservient, housewife. Or to put it another way, she was the 'good cop' in the relationship. So my mum and dad had their only son who was a bit of a disappointment in his early days. Most of the time, I felt my dad's presence over me like a very foreboding, very dark, rumbling rain cloud.

I was, at the time, always trying to please him, to keep on his good side. As I look back, it was mainly the shadows that I lived in. My memories of my starts to the day were nearly always snivelling into my cornflakes, with my dad glaring at me. Dad hated to see my cry. Not because it hurt him on a deep emotional level, but because tears from a man were simply 'not on.' He was a typical alpha male, though he didn't look like one. I mean he wasn't intimidating physically, although from a kid's perspective aged between seven and twelve, he was big enough.

He was a bully. He bullied me mostly, but also my mum and my sister. He never, ever hit either of them. That is the truth. That's why it seems to me, writing this account, slightly confusing to do justice to his character at the time. He wasn't 'full on' violent, but he had his moments, many of them, where he could be nasty and hurtful. What springs to my mind is not quite a 'baddy' in a children's animated movie, but one of the 'side kicks' not quite evil enough to have the deep, evil laugh like the baddy, but on the side and at the side of the baddy, laughing and agreeing with him.

So, many of my days started out with me feeling like s**t and hating my dad. Confused, very confused. I was only too well aware, as young children are, that I should have stopped the bed-wetting years ago. Why was I still doing it?

Years later, talking to a diabetic nurse, she told me that in her opinion, the reason I prolonged in the bed-wetting department was because I was always anxious. My dad's brooding presence was having an affect and influence on me. I think she was probably right. In fact, I heard the same thing from a child psychiatrist. Things were worse at home, parents were sick of me bed-wetting, so we went off to see a 'shrink'. Some images and memories just won't budge in a persons mind. I suppose if I had a few more 'brighter' memories, the image may have been displaced by now. I'm not sure. I was a defining part on my whole life. That's why it lingers - it has it's own omens attached to it.

Before we paid our visit to the 'shrink', my dad thought, and thought for a long time afterwards, that cold showers, beatings and name calling were the main remedies to stop me from bed-wetting. I'm glad my elder sister, and my younger sister, were never treated the same. Again, I must say that my dad was never violent to any other member of the family. He never raised a fist to my mother or sisters. Unfortunately, I was the other man in the house, and being 'a man' I think he reasoned that I could take the beatings.

Ironically, he was correct, in a very fundamental way. I was tough and hardened. He used to take me to work with him in the summer holidays, sometimes as punishment for hiding my wet things. He had a heavy toolbox and he used to make me carry it around for him. This literally amazed other people, or more importantly for me, other kids my age. So the way he treated hardened me, no doubt. I think many people are simply born as the type of person who is more likely to contract depression. People are not just born with depression. It takes some improper nurturing to bring it about.

We crave positive endorsement and reaction to keep the negative thoughts at bay. And sadly, to a very bitter extent, we can only keep those thoughts away for so long until we crave approval again. Sadly, I feel that people suffering with depression become addicted to needing to hear and feel wave after wave of positive energy. Therein lies the problem. A person isn't going to feel 'positive' all the time. That's when depressants swim with the sharks. That's when we are totally out of depth and this happens over and over again.

Between the ages of 9-12, things were probably at their worst for me in terms of wetting the bed. It feels strange writing that because I had some pretty awful days at secondary school too. It was about then that my elder sister was losing her support for me. It used to really upset her hearing me cry and tell my dad I was sorry, again and again. She never actually saw anything. She would usually be downstairs and I'd be upstairs, in the shower with cold water cascading down my back or tight against the radiator, trying to inch away from my dad's punches.

My sister was getting older and caring less about me. While I was seeing one of the 'shrinks' she had to babysit our other sister, which meant she couldn't be out with her mates. When I returned from the session, my mum and dad went for a drink and my elder sister beat me up! Not savagely or violently, just dead arms and legs. She was frustrated and embarrassed.

So, as you can guess, I wasn't too popular at home! It was about this time that my dad decided an alternative plan was required. He answered a question that I'd been pondering for quite a while. I said, "You and mum are always arguing because of me!" This included the water works and the whiny voice children make when crying. Dad agreed, wholeheartedly. That really shocked me because I wasn't expecting it. He decided to switch from physical to psychological abuse, but it totally backfired.

Dad suddenly decided the reason I was wetting the bed for years was I had a weak bladder! For years he accused me of being a 'lazy bastard,' saying that I couldn't be bothered to go to the toilet. Now, out of the blue, I'd developed a biological problem. I must admit it was a slight improvement from being labelled a 'lazy bastard.'

Things are never straightforward. I learned that very quickly. Not only did my dad have a name for my condition – incontinence - he had an answer for it as well…. an incontinent nappy! I was ten years old and my dad assured me they were only used on old people and I should, and did, feel 'acutely embarrassed.' Thankfully, he never made me where them to school - only at night, to bed. They didn't make me stop, that's for sure, and thought that was the whole point.

Dad was on a roll. Just because the nappies didn't help to stop the bed-wetting, that didn't mean he was about to give up on the idea of solving the problem. First it was discipline, and then nappies. Yet, neither of these imaginative solutions addressed the fact that the bed was wet in the morning because I slept through the whole episode. When my bladder was ready to empty at night, simply would not wake up to go to the bathroom. That was the reason. I told him then, of course, but he didn't listen to me.

A reluctant part of me believes that a part of him, my dad, enjoyed beating me. After the beatings, he'd drag me into the shower, literally throw me into place, and watch me shiver and scream as the freezing cold water drummed on my head and flowed down my naked body. He'd watch me and asked me if I thought he was enjoying doing this? My answer, between cries and sobs, was always no. Of course I didn't believe he got any enjoyment out of it. Years later, with time to reflect, I'm not so sure. I'm not suggesting that my dad, in any way, shape or form gained sexual pleasure from my humiliation. I never saw any sign of that. I believe it had more to do with control. Being the man and trying to mould me into one. I have no idea what the controlling element was, or why he felt the need to assert excessive control on a skinny little kid. I don't honestly think he knows. Mistakes are made through life; only some of them are far more costly than others.

My dad's next brainstorm was that I needed a light, a little red light, above my bed because I was afraid of the dark. Surely, a parent would have discovered years before if one of their kids was afraid of the dark? Sad thing is, I played up to the idea as I thought I might get some support. Anything to deflect the attention away from the amount of times a week that I was bringing down my wet sheets and pyjamas. The only problem was that after the instillation of the little red light above my headboard, which was on constantly all b****y night, the dam continued to leak, and the beatings continued almost on a daily basis. So my parents, at last, sought professional advice from a child 'shrink'.

I knew I should have been out mugging old ladies or swearing at innocent passers-by, enjoying myself! I can still remember the day I met with the two child psychologists. My parents were in the room - a large, spacious room which felt even bigger because its occupants were squashed into the middle of it. My dad was utterly convinced that the reason I wet the bed was my fault, not his. He told the 'shrinks' he thought it was because I was 'playing with myself'. Imagine how embarrassing it was, talking about me, masturbating, in front of two strangers and my mum.

Their expert opinion was that my dad's anger and character was making me anxious and causing me to wet the bed. If this were Hollywood, then maybe my father would have agreed that he was mainly responsible for my problems and promised to 'change his ways'. It was not Hollywood, it was Nottingham in the late seventies and early eighties. The meeting ended abruptly with my dad refusing to listen and walking out. My mum and I were forced to follow.

There was another visit, about a year or so later. This time my dad promised to try and be more understanding. A chart was constructed of days when I was 'wet' and days when I was 'dry'. I was to use to different coloured pens. It was the first time that I realised just how bad the problem was. In the space of two weeks, I'd wet the bed on twelve occasions. The deal was I brought all my wet stuff down, all the time. Also, I had to disclose to my parents the whereabouts of any hidden wet stuff.

Because I was bed-wetting at such a rate, I was forced to sleep on the floor because the mattress was drying out from the time I had soaked it! It was too much for my dad. I remember him coming to me on a day I 'flooded the banks of the Nile' and telling me he couldn't take it anymore. That's it. That's what he said. After that, it was back to the beatings, name-calling and cold showers.

So, my early years where not great. Having said that, I was lucky enough to come from a family who could and did provide me with love and a home. I had clothes to wear and food to eat. We had holidays every year, at Butlins – I have memories of my dad arguing with the accommodation manager because the chalet was too small and very damp!

Still, I honestly don't believe that my treatment as a young lad was the main reason that I find myself in this position today, constantly battling with depression. I firmly believe that people who suffer from depression suffer because they don't have the mental capacity to be able to cope. Some people, who've had it much harder, may be born with the type of character that is better able to cope with certain pressures. Having said that, the physical and mental abuse I received as a child certainly made things a hell of a lot worse. I feel the abuse made the slope even more acute. My point is I feel that sooner or later in my life, I would have encountered depression because I was born without certain coping mechanisms. My dad was "toughening me up." Perhaps he thought he was preparing me for the future.

I was petrified of my dad. He cut me down constantly with acid remarks and horrible glares. Still, I love my dad. We're not close. Then again, I'm not close to anyone anymore. He had the capacity to make me feel awful about myself, but at the same time, it was him I wanted most to please, and he who made the most effort to "cure" me. However, in keeping with me coming from, more or less, a typical family, I will now go into another facet of my childhood which has haunted me ever since. Not on the same scale as the bed-wetting, but nonetheless, it lives within my soul.

In the BBC series 'The Royal family', Antony constantly gets blamed for everything - even when he wasn't there! I was told all too often that everything - bed-wetting, nappy wearing; constant name calling by my father, punishment – it was all my fault.

I was already a sensitive boy. I wasn't tough mentally. I've never been the kind of person who can call on faith or support from his own psyche. That is very important. All those suffering from depression share this awful symptom. When things are really bad and you need to hear an inner voice-faith, echoed in confidence, all I hear, and it literally is a hearing sensation, is my father's words, used constantly against me when I was growing up: YOU USELESS LITTLE SOD or YOU PATHETIC LITTLE BASTARD. There was always an emphasis on the USELESS. When I'm struggling, my head is absolutely immersed in those thoughts.

My sisters were not treated like me, and they've turned out pretty normal. In fact, recently they've both just become mothers. I don't pretend that either of my sisters have had it smooth sailing either. Not at all! They've both had their own problems and have had the strength, mentally and physically, to cope with these problems. I love them both and I'm very proud of them. I've often wondered, for long periods of time, how they would of coped with what I went through.

My dad used to tell me that his dad was a complete bastard to him. He never went as far as saying he was beaten and put down for most of his childhood. He did recount many stories of how his dad was a 'tight arse'. He used to tell me, with a definite edge to his voice, that his dad didn't give his wife any extra housekeeping money. His dad never took his mum out or bought her any presents. His dad spent nearly all of his spare time in the pub. When my dad told me this, he didn't sound very impressed. I think it was more of a cumulative effect though. Not treating his mother well, being frugal, not affection and spending most of his free time in the local.

What used to bother me most was the stories my dad would tell about how as a 17 – 18 year old he'd pin his dad against the wall and threaten him. He didn't gloat or brag about this. Never did I detect any kind of pleasure attached to these stories. His voice was one of hurt and anger, not pride. Still, when he got to the point of pinning his dad against the wall, there was something else in his voice.

My dad had a brother. As kids growing up, my dad told me they were very close. In my dad's childhood, millions of light years ago, he had hepatitis. That meant, in his words, he had to be 'chaperoned' by his closest brother. He did have another brother, who was nine years older, and like the brother who chaperoned my father, he's now passed away. The reason I bring this brother up is because I have been

11

living in his shadow for a long time. Even though he's been dead for many years, my dad told me years ago that his brother, my uncle, was a loner. He lived on his own, never had a girlfriend and ended up dying in the house he was born in. He never left home.

When I was growing up, comparisons were made by me and funnily enough, by my dad. My dad told me once that he feared that I was going to turn out like him. As I grew older, I became painfully aware of how my life was taking a different route than that of my family and the few friends I had. I was starting to struggle with depression, though at the time I didn't know it. My friends all had relationships, be it girlfriends or boyfriends. I had barely done more than kiss a girl. My confidence was too low. It was an area of my life I hated. From the disaster that was my childhood through to the problems I encountered through my teens and early twenties, there was a knock on effect, and there was a pattern emerging.

The point is my uncle lived his whole life the way I wanted desperately to avoid. My mum says, she thinks, that it wasn't so much depression he suffered from, so much as loneliness. All I know is before the 7th December 1995, I was heading in exactly the same direction. Later, I will write about how that date had a huge affect on my life. In fact, how that day saved my life.

So I had this haunting feeling, like being followed and knowing who was following and why they were following me, up until my 23rd birthday. I feel a little guilty for having these feelings about my uncle. It wasn't his fault. He no doubt tried to change the way his life was. It isn't easy to change at the best of times, but when you're suffering from depression, you're generally a bit of a loner and you don't have an army of friends to call on for help or support. Ironically, and it's a sick, hurtful irony, sometimes you do have the friends and support in place-you just don't use them.   Another pitfall with living with depression. I'm not mute, but I suppose it must feel like not having a voice. In my experience, you simply cannot tell your friends how bad you're feeling. You will not get understanding or answers. What you will and do get is pitiful looks and wave after wave of sympathy. So you remain silent. No that's not quite true. You become a parody of yourself. You become a superb actor. In the daylight you may crack jokes and laugh at them. You nod your head at the correct times in conversation. While most of the time you are lost in questions like why me? How the hell am I going to get out of this mess? How long can I take it? How much longer can I go on?

You feel alright most of the time when you are occupied or when you're with other people. Yet, your mind still wonders and you have to slam on the brakes because if you don't, you'll be chasing after your own questions, like a dog chasing its own tail. I was turning out like my uncle because by my early twenties. I had already seen a couple of shrinks and even more councillors, and I was under pressure to change my life - drastically.

CHAPTER TWO
A FAMILY THING

My uncle was a loner. He was that kind of person. My dad is the complete opposite; loud, extrovert and flamboyant. Hours have been lost where I've been listening to him tell me, when he was younger, what 'hit' he was with the ladies! But as he tells me these things, I wonder about the pressure upon my uncle. Apparently, they went out a lot together. They were very close because my uncle had to look after my dad when he was a kid. I know from my own experience that when a quiet person is in close contact with a person with the opposite personality, it puts a lot of pressure on the naturally reticent one. You end up with jaw ache because you've been grinning and smiling, possibly all day. You don't know how else to act or react. You have nothing to say. You're thinking thoughts that completely undermine your faith and confidence. You are under so much pressure because you want to feel apart and at the same time, you don't want to appear as if you're trying to hard. This is just how it is on a daily basis, no exaggeration. A depressed person is falling without a parachute. So imagine the affect of being with somebody who is absolutely bubbling with life? It makes you feel that much worse. That's why many people suffering with depression choose to stay in. They lock themselves away because they don't want to see the rest of the world managing. You see homeless and disabled people and they appear to be coping. At least they're giving life a real go!

My uncle lived on his own in Lenton, Nottingham. He died in the house he spent most of his life. In fact, he continued to live in the same house even after his Father died. I suppose it was for practical reasons. It doesn't matter what the reasons where, he continued to live in the house long after his brothers and sister had gone, and he stayed there long after both his parents had passed away. Now that I think about it, the more it makes sense. What I know of him was that he was a quite, private person. I'm trying to avoid the word 'loner' again because it sounds cruel - like a statement, harsh in judgement and low in feeling. Perhaps he remained in the house because he could be on his own? Perhaps that's the way he wanted it. My dad often went to visit him at home or at work. I always got the impression that if it wasn't for my dad's efforts, the brothers would have drifted apart. That is a real sickening thought, because that same scenario is hovering around the fringes of my life as well.

I have very little contact with my youngest sister, who now lives in Canterbury. I have seen her twice in the past two years! My eldest sister has just moved from Nottingham to Portsmouth, within the last few weeks. When she moved back to Nottingham from Portsmouth, I saw quite a lot of her. I used to go down to her flat and we'd get drunk and sing classic songs of the 60's, 70's and 80's very loudly and mostly out of tune. Eventually, I ended up seeing less and less of her. I feel guilty because her flat was a twenty-minute walk and on most Sundays she used to come home for Sunday roast. I have no excuses to offer. I think I just grew sick of hearing about her life and the simplicity and relative ease in which she lived it. Even now, when I go home sometimes, the conversation will naturally rotate to one of her ex-boyfriends or her ex-flatmates' weddings. Or perhaps something she'd said or might say in a given situation. My point is I don't have that kind of easiness. It is strange because I'm not sure I even want it. I just feel very small and unimportant compared to my eldest sister. I have a fair understanding of psychology; I studied it for my Access To Higher Education, which was the qualification that granted me entrance into Southampton University. I know it is likely that my sister has no idea of her influence, as she lives her life exactly how she sees fit. The problem is mine, of course. As I have stated, her life has been less than simple or smooth. She is strong mentally - incredibly tough in fact. I hate arguing with her because she's one of those people who makes you lose your temper and consequently the argument. I would lay down my life for her because I love her very much. I spent so much of my early life with her and she is very dear to me.

Time to step back aboard the merry-go-round. I started to hate myself for the way I distanced myself from both sisters and my parents. It's easy to hop on the merry-go-round, as it's constantly in motion. It is easy to say that I'll open up and become less distant. I've spent so long, so many years being this character that I feel like a strange caricature or parody of myself.

What about the person suffering from depression? If the homeless and the sick and other people with physical and mental problems can get on with life, why can't we? That's when the roof falls in. The foundations of our confidence are already weak suddenly shatter. My heart is filled with a fateful concoction of hate, remorse, loathing, and frustration. I'm intelligent enough to realise that these people do have their own problems. Of course they do! But they have the facility in their conscience to believe.

They value their own thoughts and give them credence. It's a vicious, venomous circle, because the concoction of thoughts only has one destination. I then hate myself for being so weak and pathetic. For god sake if everybody else can fight and dig their way through their troubles, then why can't I?

As long as I can remember I've been fighting instead of living. What's the difference? It's hard to define, but I think I can best sum it up by stating that I have to continually tell myself that I'm a good person, that I have as much right to be on the planet as everybody else. To keep telling myself, very similar to a mantra, that things will be okay as long as I continue to believe. The major floor in this plan, and it's a hitch with the combined mass of Africa and Australia, is I don't believe in myself. I have no faith and very little confidence I have to fight and claw and dig. I survive and what gets me through is the thread, very thin that it is, that my life will be worth something. There is a reason for me to have been born and not end up the same way as the five miscarriages that my mother had before my youngest sister. That still puts a hell of a lot of pressure on my shoulders.

Whilst I was studying at Southampton University, I needed the help of a councillor. Claire was a great help to me. We got talking about my family life and I told her of my very real fear that I was turning out the same way as my uncle. I still feel guilty about referring to my dad's favourite and closest brother as a 'thing' I want desperately to avoid becoming. He was a nice bloke. He wasn't a monster. He worked all his life and died in his early fifties of cancer. It haunts me, the thought that by the time I'm fifty, like my Uncle, I'll be living alone and fighting to find my peace in the world. That thought really frightens me. I'd rather be dead than live a pointless existence on my own.

Claire, the councillor at University, told me she thought that my dad was worried, that he was anxious that I was becoming more and more like is brother and less like his son. That thought keeps me awake at night. She may be right. My dad used tell me he'd literally have to drag his brother to go out for a drink with him. I know how my uncle felt. If you're feeling low and don't want to go out, there's nothing you can do. Being out in a crowd doesn't take those thoughts away. It makes you conscious that you have to lie to yourself and those around, simply in order to fit in. The constant lying and flashing of false smiles. It drains you mentally. You feel worse because your depression is so much more apparent to you when you a wearing a false smile.

My dad does the same to me now. He is very hard to deter. His answer, as with many other people, is to socialise and relax. I try to make him understand that it's not as easy or straightforward as that. Maybe he can see his own brother in me. The comparison and similarity would be very hard not to notice. So I do worry, greatly over many years and many hours, that I will turn out to be loner, just like my uncle. However hard I try and have tried, I haven't found the simple ingredient or recipe for happiness. Though, to be honest, it's not about happiness. I want to live a normal life, where I don't feel like I have to fight or struggle through the day.

What is also very frightening is a very real sensation that my family are all advancing and progressing, while I stay exactly the same. Well, not quite the same. Unfortunately I do grow older and according to the scales, I also grow fatter! But in terms of a professional and social life, my family shift and change, and in my sisters' case, multiply. I also seem to have the same lines. I'm not at University because I'm having problems with depression. I'm not working at present because I'm experiencing one or two difficulties motivating myself. It's very, very alarming when the same excuses hold you back time and time again.

As a fairly competitive person, my life hurts all the more. I want to be a success so I can look any member of my family in the eye and feel that I can stand against them and be proud of who I am. As it is, I find it very difficult being in the same room as any member of my family because I always feel such a shit! I can't help but compare what I have achieved, or rather haven't achieved, with my two sisters and compared to my parents at my age. I know life isn't a game. Your family love you and want the best for you. However, that will not prevent me from looking at what the rest of my family have done and comparing it with what little I've achieved. Even as I think these words and then type them on my computer keypad, which is covered in dirty finger prints, I hear the thoughts in my head, and feel as if I'm bleating like a school kid who can't get his own way.

My relationship with every member of my family has definitely been affected. When I was growing up, I was really close to my eldest sister. She is two years older than me, so naturally we saw a lot of each other growing up. She used to support me through the worst times when I was having trouble with my dad because of problems with bed-wetting. She used to cry for me and, more poignantly, with me, when my dad was beating me in the mornings.

It isn't because I'm jealous or envious of my sister that our relationship has suffered. It's the same with all my family. Sometimes I feel that my life is so futile and I have made such a complete mess of it that I have nothing to contribute, not only in life, but also in terms of conversation and debate with any member of my family. I simply cannot, or find it very difficult, to look them in the eye and speak openly and honestly. I find it very hard to strike up a conversation because what do I have to contribute?

Each member of my family, like any other, have had their own personal problems to cope with. My eldest sister lost her first baby who was born prematurely. Still, she moved on and lived her life. She is now a proud mother, and within the past few weeks she's just given birth to baby Sammuel. Both my sisters have overcome their problems and are now both extremely happy. In comparison to them and what they've each been through, I feel so weak.

It isn't that I'm rude or uncivil. It is the only way that I have learned to handle those difficult and uncomfortable situations. I truly hate myself for feeling this way. Do you see? It's time to step aboard the merry-go-round again. When I have really bad days, days when I simply don't want to go out, just hide away, as I find that solitude is the best medicine. Just stay out of the public eye and lick my wounds in private. This is what I've always done - it's all I know. My family have grown accustomed to the way I live my life. My dad pesters me into going out sometime, usually a couple of hours, maybe a bit more. However, there are occasions, too many of them, that I simply will not do what I don't want to do. If I don't want to out, or even go to work, there is no point in forcing myself to go. I have learnt from experience that I feel far worse, in the public eye, a torrent of abuse and hate vibrating inside my head. My only defence, as always, is to pretend that I am fine. That I do not have any problems; that I can cope. It takes a lot more energy to be fake than it does to be alone.

A couple of years ago, my youngest sister was about to get married to Scott, her fiancé. They arranged for the whole family to go down to Canterbury for the wedding and reception. Not only were my parents, my elder sister and myself expected, but also my cousin from Cambridge. Happy occasions, weddings. My mum was like a wind up toy on overdrive. She was so excited. That's not entirely true. She was annoyed because the groom's mother was able to 'help' more because she lived in Canterbury, while my mother was stuck up in Nottingham. Still, she was very proud and incredibly excited.

About a week before the big day, I had to go into hospital and have an abscess lanced. I get them, sometimes, because I'm diabetic. Though to be honest, I was more than relieved to have this one because it provided me with just the excuse I was looking for. I don't expect it would be a great surprised to reveal that I didn't want to go to the wedding. I was, again, feeling really low.

I consulted my doctor after I'd got out of hospital. I explained my situation, and she nodded her head at the right times and offered me sympathy. She then doubled the dose of anti-depressants I was taking and wished me luck in telling my mother. I was really hoping for some kind of magic wand effect. Or better still, that she would tell my mother! I have to admit, I was scared. All my years as a kid growing up, it has always been my dad's temper or my mum telling me 'wait until your dad gets home from work'. On this occasion it was my mother who I desperately wanted to avoid. She was organising what clothes I would wear and my dad. She was on overdrive, brimming with expectation and pride about the wedding, and I was going to have to tell her that I couldn't make it!

I arrived home from the doctors and found my dad sitting down in the rocking chair in the living room. That was, when I was growing up, the posh room, where we had small parties and entertained the odd guest. The front room was where the television was. I told him the doctor had more than doubled my dose of anti-depressants, or 'happy pills'. Honesty is sometimes the best policy, but not always! I told him that the abscess on the top of my thigh still wasn't healing properly. In fact, it was still leaking a small amount of fluid, but not enough to prevent me from going to the wedding. His reply was something along the lines of 'well if you can't go, you can't go'. As simple as that. I felt guilty about lying so I also told him I couldn't face the happy faces and enthusiasm. He nodded and said it was understandable. We both agreed to tell my mother that I couldn't travel because of my leg. I felt a mixture of incredible relief and absolute hate for myself.

Even now, well over a year since the wedding, it still 'gets to me'. Not the thought of ruining this special day, but the thought of being all dressed up and pretending to be happy at the wedding. Why should I have to pretend anything? It's a happy occasion and I am not a happy person. For the sake of my sister, I should have found strength from somewhere and 'dug in'. It was only a weekend. Still, what concerned me more was how I would react when I returned from the weekend if I went. Having to pretend for a whole weekend that all was well would have been intolerable - hating myself for having to physically force myself to laugh or smile, when all the while I was feeling the complete opposite.

I would of come home and remained a prisoner in my room. Absolutely tormenting myself with all the happy images and comparing them with this thing that stares back at me in the mirror. That's what really concerned me, the loathing I'd have for myself as a I compared my life, my image, with everybody else's.

This is definitely one time I can categorically claim that depression and my family clashed, big time! I took my father into my confidence and told him how I really was feeling. I can honestly say that I didn't lie. I told him the doctor advised that I didn't travel down there and she did prescribe double the normal amount of 'happy' pills. All true. I also told my dad how low I was feeling at the time. As soon as my mum and dad walked through the door and my dad sat in his rocking chair, the one that doesn't rock too smoothly, my mum fixed her stare on me and told me she was disappointed with me. She had every right. It was her youngest daughter's wedding day.

I couldn't go. It was simple as that. Yet, my mother simply wasn't prepared to listen to any argument that I had to offer. As far as she was concerned, I had let my little sister down and she made it very clear that there was nothing I could ever do to make up for it! I told her that I didn't plan any of it. I wanted to go but there was no way I was going to pretend for the whole weekend. What she didn't realise was the damage it can do, I mean after the event. Weeks, maybe even months later, images of how bad I felt and how I lied and faked my way through the occasion would have haunted me. I couldn't do it. I still feel ashamed and guilty. My mother was right. I had let myself and the family, and more importantly, my little sister down, but if the same thing happens tomorrow, at this moment in time, I will do the same. It's hard enough coping with reality without having to live life as a fake, pretending to be happy when you're not.

I was so angry and frustrated with arguing with my mum, that I forgot to be angry with my dad for telling her in the first place! Most importantly, though, my sister forgave me. What's to forgive, though? I still angers me now. I didn't host a party or hold the world's largest orgy. While they were all down there, I was in Nottingham threatening the cat!

My life was pretty much summed up by hiding away, not facing my problems. Not that simple though. I wish it were. If it were as simple as facing the crowds, then I wouldn't be bleeding my heart out now. I think my mother understands now. She's had so many years to get used to it. She knows how I handle my difficult moments.

So the bottom line is, I feel ashamed to be with my family. That really tears me apart because none of us are getting any younger. As long as I feel that I am worthless and have nothing to live for, sadly, I don't see how things can change. I hope I'm wrong. I really do.

There was a time, in 1994. I was still suffering from depression. You know, that is a real worry. It seems every time I look back, it's with a wince, or it's as if I know there something nasty hiding behind the curtain and I grimace and pull the fabric back very slowly because I'm afraid of what I might see! My elder sister had just lost her young baby son, Jake Everton Baines - I love that name. Her boyfriend at the time was a huge Everton fan. She phoned home and gave my mother news of the baby's death. She asked to speak to me and said she wanted me at the funeral. I wanted to travel up to North Wales and attend a funeral about as much as I wanted to run naked down our street. She was adamant, though, she wanted me there and I agreed to go.

I went with my mother on the train. I really wasn't looking forward to it. I don't mean to sound callous or cold-hearted. Nobody looks forward to funerals. What I mean is, as usual, I wasn't working, had piled on the weight and felt very uncomfortable in the public eye. I wasn't used to being out in public. That's always a major factor in my depression. I don't really see it as comfort eating. I don't gain any comfort from it. It's a vicious circle. I feel very low, worthless. Can't see a future so I think to myself, 'what is the point in looking good if I don't feel good'? I hide away and eat and eat. I look in the mirror and hate the person I see for a number of reasons. Firstly, I've put on weight, so my clothes don't fit me and I have to wear baggy sweatpants. More than hating the image physically is the fact that mentally I've been defeated. I hate the way I look. Hate myself for allowing my body to fall into disrepair and worse, like scythe swinging threateningly, I yet again prove I don't have the mental strength to combat depression; in short, I'm on my knees again.

Usually what happens when I'm at the stage of hating what I see in the mirror is like a tongue seeking out that bad tooth. I know it's a cliché but it's a very accurate way of recounting how my mind tortures itself. I'd go on and mentally or verbally list all the great things my sister had achieved, even though they have had to negotiate problems as well. I think about how my parents are proud of my sisters and embarrassed by me. And on and on it goes, until I feel absolutely shattered.

Going to my sister's baby's funeral was a different matter though. It wasn't like it was going to be a party atmosphere. I wasn't going to find myself trapped in a situation in which I was smothered by smiling, happy faces and wall-to-wall laughter. Of course, I knew it was going to be a sombre affair, full of tears, remorse and bitterness. I went because my sister wanted me to go. I'd like to think it was because we were, at that time, pretty close. Again I was very low, overweight and very paranoid about being out of my own room. My father didn't come and it was only years later that I learned, from my sister, that my youngest sister wanted to attend, but she was told she was not allowed. So it was just me and my mother on the train to Ryhl, North Wales.

When I arrived and spoke with my sister, she told me the reason she wanted there, especially me, was because she knew how low I was feeling. 'Low' is a very poor definition of just how bad I was feeling at that time. I remember the night the phone call came. It was just me and my dad in the front room. We were watching a repeat of 'Cracker'. It was something that we did together, watch Cracker. I told him how bad I was feeling; how utterly miserable I was. I told him I'd had enough. I wanted to die. I was going to kill myself. I remember his reaction shocked me. He was very calm and relaxed. His reply was something like, 'If that's how you feel.' I like to think he didn't take me very seriously. I think he simply thought that I was crying for help. So I was very low at this time and the last thing I really wanted to do was travel to North Wales with my mum and watch my sisters baby being buried. Still, my sister wanted me to be there, and I wanted to be there for my sister.

On the train to Wales I attempted to make 'polite' conversation with my mother. I know it wasn't easy for her either. How could it have been? Her son didn't want to go and her first-born had lost her son. I was very difficult for my mother.

So the reason my sister wanted me at the funeral was because she wanted me to witness, first-hand, what it was like to see people suffering at a funeral. She wanted me to imagine that it was my funeral and people were crying and mourning for me. She wanted me to see the emotional damage and devastation a loss of life inflicts on those left behind. But so much worse, was a loss of life by suicide. The loss to those left behind is unbearable. I didn't exactly thank her for her comments. I didn't really know what kind of reaction to offer her. I was shocked, even speechless.

It was an incredible day, one that I'll never forget. Of course it was awful. Sad and pointless. My sister is very much like my father. They both speak their mind, and they're both very lively, animated people. They get straight to the point. After the funeral, everybody went to the local pub, the Ty Fry. As soon as everybody walked in, the nervous conversation gathered pace and people were hopping from one foot to the other and not sure what to do with their hands or eyes. My sister came up to me, gave me a pound coin and told me to put some 'lively' music on the juke box. I awkwardly agreed. As soon as the music came on, people started to relax. I suppose like me, they felt guilty about it. My sister wanted her baby to be celebrated as much as possible. She didn't want tears or sadness. She told my dad she preferred the idea of the 'Irish wake' and hated the thought of people crying on her shoulder all day.

The pub actually ran dry of Guinness. There was laughter and smiles. We said that Jake had a really good send off. I've never, to this day admired or been as proud of a person in equal quantities. My sister had done her crying in private. She wanted to be strong and my God she was. On that day I literally forgot about my problems because my sister sucked the life out of me. I don't know how else to describe it. She made me very proud to even know her, never mind be related to her. She was so strong mentally that I felt weakened standing by her. I didn't for one moment feel envious or jealous that she oozed absolute strength. Remember, Little Jake was buried. His coffin was about a foot long. As my sister watched her boyfriend at the time carry the coffin towards the hole, all eyes were attracted to her. She was pinned to the spot by hundreds of pairs of obtrusive eyes. She started straight ahead and not a tear passed her eyes. I felt so tall, so powerful. I was related to this incredible young girl. I will also mention the fortitude of her boyfriend. He had to carry the little coffin. He held it so delicately; so carefully. He didn't raise his eyes when he knew he was the focus of everybody's attention. He was incredible.

It's only now, ten years later, that I feel any bitterness or anger about that day. It was a monumental day, one that I'll never forget. I could have made it count. I feel I should have learned from that day and gone on to become a better person. Because standing in the pub, with the rest of the mourners, trying not to tap our feet to the loud music, I felt stronger than I had felt for many years. Empowered is what comes to mind. I felt that I could go on and actually do something with my life. Now, as I think about the last four or five years, I feel like striking out in anger. My sister was so brave and now look at me, moaning, bleating. I can't formulate a clear strategy because I spend so much time hating myself.

So I continue to live in fear of becoming the mirror image of an uncle who I hardly even knew. It terrifies me to think that my relationship with my father is more like the relationship he had with his brother. The older I get, it seems the narrower the parameters of the tunnel become. I have less and less options. I keep making the choices and decisions that push me closer and closer to becoming the person I don't want to be. Maybe I'm just panicking. The longer my life goes on, the more I feel like a fish, slowly being reeled in. I have struggled and fought to get off the hook, but I always seem to end up out of work, out of love and totally lost at sea.

What hurts the most, I think, is not being able to stand up tall and proud against my dad. Of course, the same can be said of my relationship with my mother. I can't help but compare myself to sisters and even my cousins. I have nothing to boast about. I have not really been anywhere or done anything. No, that's not quite true. It just that I haven't achieved anything that I'm comfortable with. I know my parents love me, but I have or had, a burning, raging passion to make them proud of me. The truth is I haven't given them anything gloat or boast about. Fine, I was the first in our family to go to University but would you be shocked to learn that I only lasted three months?

The ramifications of that event just get added onto the accumulator. I find it even harder to face my parents now, especially as they both told me how proud they were of me. The thought of their words and the look on their faces still haunts me. I loved it, at the time. I was the one under the spotlight. I had the attention. It was my turn to shine. It was the chance that I always wanted. So now, when I go home, I have to force myself to forget. Put their praise and compliments out of my head. It's hard not to torment myself, because I feel I deserve it. I deserve to suffer because I have let so many people down. Yes, I suppose the worst part is that I let myself down. It's even worse when you let your parents down. I feel whatever I say now has no validity, no credence. How can it have? I was the boy who boasted about going to University. My parents, to their credit, never mention it.

I feel like I am drifting further and further away from reality and life, and ultimately, my family. It seems I've been saying and thinking the same things for years now. I'm sick of being on my own. I want a steady relationship. I want to feel that I have some role to play in life. I want to live and not fight or dig in my heels and hang onto life. I have been saying these things for the last ten years at least. It is very sobering to think that nothing has changed in that space of time. Small, insubstantial things may have changed around me, but I have inevitably remained the same.

When I was sixteen or seventeen, I had just started to enjoy the benefits of going out and drinking in pubs. My parents have always been very liberal and they told me that they knew I was going to do it anyway. My sister and I where really close at this point. She had just left school and I was just about too. My dad used to meet us at the local pub called the Porchester and time used to fly. I loved that part of my life. I was young and proud. I was always in the toilets 'doing' my hair or making sure I stood opposite a mirror. I honestly felt at that time that my dad was proud of me. I appeared confident and I had that arrogance that young lads have. The swagger and manner of one who expects great things from life. I had also started to weight train with my dad at a local gym. It was something else that bonded us closer together. I suppose, sadly, this time is the closest that I've ever felt to my dad. His treatment of me in the past never came up. I didn't want to argue with him. To bring up 'that' subject would have caused an awkward reaction.

I love my family. I wish I could feel closer to them. I want my parents to be proud of me. I suppose they are, but I feel their pity as well. They know how I feel and can't do anything for me. I feel I'm being reeled in, just like my uncle.

CHAPTER THREE
HOLIDAYS

I remember, as a young kid growing up, feeling really frustrated and envious of most of schoolmates. You see, they would go to what at the time seemed exotic locations in and around Spain for holiday. They would come back to school looking incredibly brown. In fact, I always suspected they had in fact, done the same as me and lied about the location of their 'fabulous' holiday and slapped a bottle or two of fake tan on! If you went to Skegness, you told everybody at school that you went to a hot place in Portugal that you couldn't remember the name of. The same applied to Mablethorpe or Cornwall.

Image is everything at school and you would try pretty damn hard to 'outdo' your mates. Sadly, for me, my mates would bring back photos of the place or really useless presents or souvenirs. That made it impossible for me to lie, unless I went to really extraordinary lengths. I always dreamed of going to Spain or somewhere else my mates had been, not for any cultural benefit, but because I wanted to go abroad was so I could bring back an useless memento and challenge my mates to get any practical use from it! So everybody knew I spent my main holiday either at my

Grandma's in Haverhill, Cambridge or at that famous UK resort, Butlins.

By the time we were holidaying as a family, my little sister must have been about four or five. I was eleven or twelve and my eldest sister was thirteen or fourteen. It was especially hard for my eldest sister. She had started drinking by the time she was fourteen and the time spent with her family, one or two weeks away in usually Butlins or possibly, slightly better, Grandma's was like a severe prison sentence to her. My little sister loved it, of course. On most holiday snaps she is the little one with ice cream all over her face and grinning insanely at the camera. My elder sister would usually stay out of the photos, unless it meant teasing me or my younger sister! There is a brilliant picture of my youngest sister, on the wall of a fountain and somebody, probably a bored young lad away with his family, putting washing powder into the fountain. So there is foam bubbling away and it is frothing all over the place. My sister is screaming because she is scared of the foam and my dad is turned towards the camera laughing! My eldest sister took the photo.

My bed-wetting didn't confine itself to Nottingham. My life and my holiday would have been much more relaxing and simple if that so called God had done me a favour and made sure the bladder went on another holiday! It was much worse to bed wet away from home, on holiday, because my mother and father wasted no time in letting me know that part of their leisure time was not supposed to be washing my sheets etc. I could see their point, but I didn't exactly get much fun out of it either.

I went through a stage, when I was younger, where I wasn't aloud to drink after 8 p.m. This, combined with taking some horrible medicine, was designed to have some affect on my bed-wetting. I used to sneak a few biscuits in my dressing gown pocket so I could have something to take away the vile taste of this 'devils brew.'

One of my cherished memories from a pretty torrid childhood was the journey to the holiday. My dad was a self-employed electrician and he drove around in a little Ford van. It was a purely utilitarian van. It had a driver's seat and a passenger seat and in the rear it had the space of roughly two square meters. If this vehicle belonged to my mother, she would have placed all the tools in the back in a regimented and clear fashion. "A place for everything and everything in its place" she would say. Most importantly, the tools and equipment would 'look nice and smell very sweet'. She would have potted plants and pot puree.

The point is my dad had to spend hours, usually the day before the journey, clearing out his tools, spending hours looking for tools that should have been there, sweeping out and then hovering the inside of the van. When all his tools and equipment were strewn across the lawn or on the floor, my sisters and I would then make the inside more comfortable We would use quilts and big cushions and also the odd pillow. A fairly easy, straightforward job would usually end up with either one of us falling out with the other two or more often than not, all of using falling out with each other.

So that's how we'd travel to our destination. I was really comfortable in the back. My little sister would 'throw a mardy' because my eldest sister and me would have the positions that offered the view from the back windows. Whilst travelling there, life didn't seem so bad. I could look out of the back window and watch the world zoom by. Even then, I was learning to try and make the most of those peaceful times. I knew I'd wet the bed. It was absolutely guaranteed. The problem with wetting the bed on holiday was that there was no way to hide the sheets. I would have to share a room with somebody and my mother, always my mother, would check the sheets in the morning.

Things would go pretty smoothly when we first arrived. We would locate the chalet, and usually find it was damp or stunk. My dad would complain and get us another chalet. For me, everything was done at breakneck speed. I was pretty excited when we'd first arrive because I hadn't done anything wrong yet. Nothing could be my fault so I felt pretty good about the world. I would be cocky and swagger. Even then, as a kid, I think I was more astute and intelligent than I gave myself credit for. I was pretty sure that the following morning I would wake up with a wet bed and receive accusations of ruining the holiday for everybody and generally be badmouthed by my dad. So my favourite part of the holiday was the Saturday we arrived.

We'd usually arrive by late morning or early afternoon. After unpacking the van and putting the gear in our rooms, my mother would make us all lunch, which would usually be cobs or rolls with cheese or ham and crisps. The rest of the afternoon was spent walking around, or for me, bombing around like in insane lunatic while my family strolled around taking in the sites. We were given a map and on the map, and on the map were locations to the certain attractions. Map reading and my mother didn't add up so my dad would take responsibility of leading us on our expedition. At times like this I really felt part of the family. It felt like I was in a family, as part of a family unit, and not the catalyst for endless arguments.

What I recall, very vividly from our holidays at Butlins, was that we always opted to go self-catering. The chalets, along with their damp patches and distinctly odd odour, provided kitchens and fridges. I remember the fridge always being stocked with all kind of delights, including chocolate! I remember once at Minehead I spent the whole week playing football all mornings. It was a special coaching session presented by an ex-professional footballer. I had forgotten to pack my shorts so I had to play all the matches and all the coaching sessions in jeans.

I can remember, even now, going out at night on my own. My sister and I were given an allowance each. I spent most of mine on the arcades and buying chips and cakes and chocolate. The last night at Minehead I particularly recall because my parents and elder sister had a huge argument about her staying out late. They didn't like the time she came in or the people she was socialising with. I was the complete opposite. I remember I had made a few mates, but tended to spend time on my own, just drifting around the arcades and stuffing my face with food.

I felt like crap on that holiday. I remember sneaking back to the chalet and raiding the fridge. I ate packets of chocolate bars. That's the first time I can associate a low feeling, with symptoms of depression. I do it all the time now. I try not to, but sometimes I think 'what the hell' and eat myself into oblivion. I remember mounting a severe assault on the contents of the fridge and then simply drifting around outside. I'm pretty sure I wasn't suicidal. I just knew I was really unhappy.

I remember one incident on holiday which showed my dad in a different light. I was off, on my own, playing crazy golf. The deal is, you give your chalet key as a deposit and in return you're handed the equipment. I lost the ball under a hedge and went and told the person in charge of handing out all the equipment. He refused point blank to give me a new ball, even though behind him was a basket full of yellow golf balls. I went home and told my dad what happened and he huffed and puffed and told me he would get me a new game. When we arrived at the little hut, I pointed to the man sitting down reading the paper. My dad explained the situation and then the man stood up. He was huge. His dimensions were impressively wide as they were tall. He diplomatically refused me another game and my dad agreed with him. Walking away, with our backs to the little shed, my dad looked down at me and asked me why I hadn't told him that the man was so big. To be honest, I didn't know he way, as he was sitting down during my brief conversation with him. It made me realise that my dad wasn't as tough as he made himself out to be.

I had a nasty surprise when we got back from that holiday. The morning we left for holiday, I'd woken up with wet sheets and pyjamas, but didn't say anything. I didn't want to start the first day of my official holiday by having to march downstairs and get in trouble for wetting the bed. Though to be honest, my dad was too busy making sure the van was working alright to spend time hitting me. It was my holiday and I wanted to feel good! When we arrived home a week later, my mother decided to put fresh sheets on my bed. The room must have stunk and the sheets must have been stained. I got a good hiding from my dad and my mum was really angry too. I was accused of feigning illness on the way to Minehead, when all the time I was feeling guilty about wetting the bed. So I had a pretty crap holiday and worse was to follow when I got home.

I remember when I was younger, I was wetting the bed to such an extent that my parents had told me they were worried about me going on holiday with them. There was only my eldest sister and I at the time, so I would have been between six and seven. We were all at the breakfast table and I had wet the bed and my dad was, as usual, upset with me. He said unless I stopped wetting the bed, I was not to go on holiday with the rest of the family. Of course, asking me to stop wetting the bed was like asking water not to be wet! It was a cruel thing to do, although I'm sure now that there was never any real intention of not taking me along with the rest of the family. I, of course, didn't know that at the time.

For me, spending the entire summer break at my Grandma's was something to look forward to because, and I feel guilty to have to admit it, my dad wasn't there. As I have grown older I have seen him change, transform into a softer, more understanding man. But years ago, when I was young enough to spend the summer in Haverhill, I was terrified of him. As father and son, we were not close and I knew it. I cannot state with absolute certainty, but I'm pretty sure that my 'wet' days were drastically reduced at my grandma's. I was blamed for everything ' in our house'. There was always an 'edge' to my dad's viciousness. He made me feel like crap. He looked at me like dirt and I honestly wondered at times whether or not I actually was his son. My reasoning for this was because he seemed to hate me, a lot of the time. I thought maybe I was adopted and he wanted to send me back to the orphanage. I've checked my birth certificate a number of times.

So when I was at my Grandma's, I was probably the person I should have been at home. I mean I had more confidence and I was less surly. Knowing that I wasn't going to get blamed for things which I hadn't done did a lot for my confidence. I felt more relaxed and much less on edge. I realise that wetting the bed in your grandma's house isn't the best way to endear yourself to a grandparent. Both my Grandma and Granddad let it be known that they were disappointed with me, but they never punished me or called me names. That was the big difference. I felt angry and disappointed with myself. I had let myself down.

However, everything was more relaxed there. I naturally felt awkward for a while afterwards, but it didn't take long before I was bombing around outside with my cousins. I suppose my grandparents' reactions may have been different because they didn't have to put up with me on a permanent basis. I wonder, even now, how they would have reacted if I lived with them for a whole year? Would they have been as patient and as understanding? The environment was totally different. Much softer and kinder. I didn't feel as if my back was up and at any moment I was going to hear my dad or mum calling out my name. There were, or there seemed to be dark, sinister, foreboding anchors attached to their voices, every time they called my name. This could be because I had hidden some sheets or other wet clothes somewhere and they'd been discovered. Or it might be because I had broken something, hadn't owned up to it and was anxiously awaiting my name to come echoing down the street. I admit, I was my own worse enemy most of the time. However, most crimes and consequent punishments revolved around wetting the bed, and I don't hold myself wholly responsible for those occasions.

So it is perhaps understandable why I enjoyed going to my Grandma's most summers. There is one absolutely horrible memory that refuses to die. My grandma's taste in music is more haunting than any childhood memory I recall. She'd sometimes make my sister and I, and perhaps a poor cousin or two, sit on the back doorstep, always on sunny days and listen to ...Cliff Richard! I still know all the words to 'Carry doesn't live here anymore'! However much I mock the music or the memories, I have to admit, they were fun. It always strikes me as funny even to this day, that my grandma would only play the music on a sunny day. It what as if she was claiming that the weather was influenced by Cliff Richard!

Time at my Grandmas was always better for me than it was for my elder sister. My mother's mother is the grandma I refer to. My mother's sister and brother still lived in the area and their kids, my cousins, lived near my Grandmas. I was lucky enough to have a cousin who was only a couple of years younger than me and this cousin had a brother who was only a couple of years younger than him. I suppose I was the leader of our little gang. My elder sister didn't really have anyone to hang around with. From what I can recall, at first, she played with the three of us. Problem was, of course, she was a girl in an exclusively boys club!

Many years before this, my elder sister and I were staying with my Grandma and it was decided that the two of us would go and stay with my Grandma's sister for a few days. I remember that when we were together, we could be little angels. On the other hand, my sister had a wicked influence on me and we often got into real trouble. We were both a little apprehensive about this visit to my Grandma's sisters. Depending on who they're with, whether it is a teacher or parent, kids know what buttons to press to get certain reactions. With my Grandma we had to be careful. She appeared soft and easy to handle, but like many of these types of characters, she had a quick temper and it was best to avoid it if at all possible.

So when we arrived at our destination, we were quite relived to learn that my grandmother was going to stay with us for the weekend. That changed our attitudes and consequently influenced our behaviour. I cannot admit to remembering anything about this stay, apart from on the Saturday we arrived, my Grandma shoved my sister and I into doing a 'talented kids' competition

I say 'shoved' because I distinctly remember that neither my sister nor I was actually asked if we would like to enter the competition. If we were asked, I'm sure the answer would have been 'no'. The task was very simple: to get up on stage and look as 'cute' as possible while trying to divert attention from the fact that we couldn't actually sing! Fortunately for me, my Grandma made sure that the microphone was set at my sister's height, which meant I had to stand on my tiptoes the whole of the performance. On the photos, on a scale of one to ten on the 'cute' score, I have to admit, were pretty near perfect. The song we were forced into singing was 'tie a yellow ribbon' - another one of my

Grandma's favourite songs. Incredibly, we were relegated to second place by an even sweeter performance, by a little girl in pigtails, holding a cuddly teddy bear! My Grandma and her sister logged a complaint. They claimed we were the most talented performers on display! We still finished second.

The lasting memory of this stay revolved around a fridge and strawberry flavoured jelly. My Grandma's sister lived in a caravan. Or she was staying on a caravan site when we went to visit. My sister was about six and I was about four. It was raining outside and we had our lunch and were given the strawberry jelly as desert. I'm not sure how it is for other brother and sister relationships, but when it came to my sister and me, she was always the catalyst. When my Father's dad, Granddad, used to come to our house for Sunday lunch, my mother used to prepare, in the 'dining' room, which is otherwise known as the room without the television in it, and the one used for 'posh' occasions. She would spend hours cooking off meats and preparing the salad. My dad and granddad would be at the pub and my mum spent most of her Sunday afternoon running around for everybody else. The food was set out on the kitchen top. The long, sideboard, which looked like it was made from marble, but it, was much cheaper material than that. The table was prepared with tablemats, posh glasses and the knives and forks. You could tell this was 'posher' event than usual, because there was a clean, mainly white tablecloth, covering the entire table.

At my Grandma's sisters we had been pretty well behaved throughout the weekend. Maybe we thought that by being forced to sing on stage, we had earned the right to create a little mayhem. I'm not sure why we did it, but I remember, even now, more than twenty-five years later, it was fun! My sister must have been bored with eating the jelly, because she carefully placed the wobbly red jelly on the end of her spoon and turned the spoon around and catapulted the jelly at the gleaming white surface of the fridge. We then took turns catapulting the rest of the jelly against the white fridge. We both thought it was great fun! That was until my Grandma and her sister suddenly appeared.

Those moments are special to me because they were at a time when depression had no influence on me at all. I was my own person and never had the opportunity to blame or use depression as an excuse. But today, I feel I always use depression as the first line of defence, largely because I can't think of anything better.

When I was younger I would sometimes travel with my dad, all over the country. He was a self-employed electrician and he found that he could get better-paid jobs outside Nottingham. Sometimes during the holidays, it was decided by my parents that a suitable punishment for wetting the bed and lying was to go to work with my dad. I used to love being away from the house. Unfortunately for me, because a lot of the work my dad took was outside Nottinghamshire, it would mean a long car journey. Remember that I was being punished (again) so we were not exactly chatting like a couple of buddies. There was mostly long, difficult silences. As the day ate into the hours, it would be as if he'd forgotten that I was there to be punished. I was actually a valid worker at those times. I would carry his toolbox and fetch his tools. Ironically, they were nice moments between my dad and I. My father and I had such a bad start to our relationship that any good, happy memories that I recall are very important.

I remember one of my jobs was to clean all the mugs with sand! Sand is actually an excellent stain remover! The building site we were on was the bare structure of houses, bricks and mortar but no glass for the window frames. By the end of the afternoon, my work consisted of standing on the top of one of the buildings and being shot at by an imaginary gun. I would then clutch my wound and fall off the roof as dramatically and theatrically as I could. A huge pile of sand cushioned the impact and I'd laugh so hard. Not to be outdone my dad insisted that have his turn. We ended playing for ages. That was a perfect day for me. I'll treasure it and take it with to the grave.

At my Grandma's I didn't turn into a saint or a wonder child. I still made mistakes and if I were bad I'd get some kind of punishment. I could live with that. I think, even all those years ago, I was intelligent enough to realise that if you're bad and you're caught, you have to 'pay' for what you have done. At home it was always different. I always felt like I was being followed by a black rain cloud. Whenever something was broken, I immediately felt under threat. It's hard to explain exactly how I felt growing up at home. Yet, I had none of this feeling at my Grandma's. I felt so much more relaxed and confident. It still mattered, but it just didn't eat into my heart. So going home was so much more meaningful to me. I'm not sure that I felt the same way at the time. I can make these comments now, obviously knowing what happened. I feel that I realised my role in the family shifted at my Grandma's. At home, I was the 'difficult' or troublesome one.

As I was approaching my 16th birthday and my elder sister was approaching her 18th birthday, my Grandma used to hold these family gatherings. They were huge events. The house was only a small council house yet somehow, we'd fit all my family in – that's five of us. My mothers' brothers family was four more. My mothers' sisters family added another four. Plus my grandparents! My dad looked completely as ease with my mother's side of the family. He was then, and still is a friendly, social person. Still, it must have been a little daunting not to have any of his family around him.

For some reason, not too many years after that, in my early teens, I really started to suffer from depression. I look back at those parties, only in memory. I cannot watch the videos taken of us at these parties as I look so happy and confident. Roughly, at the time of these parties I had stopped wetting the bed for around two years. That made me overdose on confidence, and I'm sure it was a contributing factor to my depression.

CHAPTER FOUR
SCHOOL DAYS

I loved junior school, most of the time. I was quite a popular kid and had that 'cocky' swagger' that movie stars, sports stars and cocky young school kids. It's important that I make it clear that I'm not about to contradict myself. I like to think, even now, I didn't carry my problems with me - most of the time. My dad used to tell me that because of the way he treated me, I would be one of the toughest kids in school. He was probably right in terms of hardness physically. I was tough. There is always a hierarchy at any institution, be it a school or any other environment. I was never the hardest or the best fighter, but it was generally known that I wasn't soft. I was not one of those 'fat wheezy, bespectacled kids', whose mothers forbade playing any contact sport. I was never part of the chess club!

As I was to find out, at my own expense: being robust is not just about physicality. Looking back, as I often do, I would swap my proud record of being one of the boys who you didn't mess with, to being hardened mentally. To be able to cope with those days that, at the time, I just assumed I was having a bad day. It is a quality that I have a huge amount of respect for.

As I've intimated earlier, a huge part of life at the time, roughly between the ages of 9-13, was 'getting away' with hiding my wet sheets and bedclothes. If only, with accordance with my Hollywood film in mind, life is like the movies! I could have brought my wet 'stuff' down in the mornings, even cracked a joke with my old man, while happily tucking into my cereals and toast at the breakfast table, which was vibrating with laughter and effervescence. Do I sound bitter? I feel bitter!

No it wasn't like that. If I was dry, I was much more confident. It seems cruel and very unfair now, as I think of what little it took to fill me with confidence. Just being able to go down stairs in the morning and face both my parents, without having to walk past them, squeezing by them, so I didn't contaminate them with contact from my wet things. It would, nine times out of ten, mean that the day was going to be very good. Or at least have the chance of being very good.

As I'd get hit and given a cold shower whether I told the truth or not, I reasoned that I may as well not hide the stuff - what difference would going to make? As it happened, it made a great deal of difference. Firstly in terms of my punishment, once my crime was discovered. If it was a sunny day and my mother didn't have time to check my room, there was a good chance that my sheets would dry and I would not be found out! The problem with this scenario was it was very bad on my nerves. In the morning I'd be okay. I'd laugh and joke and try and get work done. In the afternoon, from lunchtime until the final bell -it was agony. I'd be to worried about having to walk through the door and face my mother.

It definitely affected my performance at school. My mind was always elsewhere, wondering, hoping that I could get away with hiding my 'stuff' again. It used to take me ages to walk home. I know it's just my mind playing tricks on me, but it honestly always felt like I was walking under a permanent rain cloud. It would seem that I'd become immune to smiling or happiness. I write 'walk' home. I was plodding home. It was of a time when a young person could be on their own and feel relatively safe. Yes I plodded and meandered, taking the longest possible route. The image, if not the sensation will never leave me. As I walked onto my road, school jumper hanging around my waist and tie scrunched up into my pocket, the first thing I did was to walk into the centre of the road and try and locate my bedroom window. My bedroom was at the front of the house and the position of the window, even now, gives me chills.

If the window were open, it meant that my mother had found my wet things and she was airing the room. If it was closed, 99 times out of 100 it would mean I was in the clear. I used to hate the approach to my road. Looking back, this is where I learned to be a good liar. I would be walking with my mates, listening to their laughter or voices. I'd nod my head and agree with whatever they were talking about, fitting in and not wanting to look out of place or appear different. Inside, I'd prepare myself to see the window – would it be open or closed? Hoping and promising a God I never truly believed existed or had any faith in that I was going be a good follower, if only the window was closed. The relief I felt if the window was closed was incredible.

On the other hand, if it were open I'd freeze. Not physically, I may still be in front of my friends. No my heart would freeze and then after a few moments I would plod up the drive and stand around outside. I recall doing it in the rain. I was building up my courage - psyching myself up -it took a lot of doing because I am, and was then, a bloody coward. What if my sister wasn't home? What if she saw me hanging around? She'd know what the problem was. Worse still, what if my dad arrived home while I was busy steeling myself for what was inevitably to come? It was a horrible situation to be in. I went through this process time and time again. I waited outside and then suddenly like a demonic wave, I would have a panic attack. The thoughts involving my sister and father, both arriving home at the same time. Sending me over the edge and through the front door.

I always remember shutting the door so quietly, like it was made of china. Holding my breath and standing still on the carpet that you were supposed to wipe your feet on. I'd just stand still. Somehow, in my mind, I worked out it was better that I find my mother and not the other way around. Had I had just handed the wet stuff over in the morning, I would not have to go though this agony. Ironically, my mother would never really make a fuss of what I'd done. She'd tell me she was disappointed in me and shake her head. We both knew that nothing was ever resolved until my dad was home from work.

Usually, it just so happened that the evenings that I would have to tell my dad what I'd done always seemed to be the ones where I had to sit around and wait for him to come home from work. So a lot of the time, he'd arrive home late, already in a foul mood and then pretty much as soon as he stepped foot through the door, I'd give him the good news.

My school years weren't all bad. There were loads of times that I recall were I really enjoyed life. My father's mother sister lived in Mansfield - a small town, not thirty miles away from Nottingham. Strange place this, because, even though it's very close to Nottingham, it is completely different. The accent hits you straight away. It is very broad and really strong. It always sounds to me like a 'proper' northern accent. Anyway, my father's aunts, Phyllis and Lillie, lived here. One of the aunts, I cannot remember which one, had a son, Bryan, who was totally crazy. When you're ten, what you desperately want is for one of your relatives to be insane! It really makes life interesting! We used to travel there on a Sunday, same time of year, every year for about four or five years. It was an old mining village and what I recall of the people was that they were really friendly. We went up, me and my sister, and dad. My mum would be at home, looking after my little sister.

I felt better, more relaxed when I was out of the house. As I mentioned in the first chapter, things were having an accumulative affect on me. I was the 'black sheep' in the family. I hated being blamed for everything. I also despised being called 'useless' by my dad. At home, I felt trapped. I honestly felt like I couldn't escape. When I was out with my mate, especially if I was in the clear at home, I could walk down the road, approach the window and it have no affect on me. They were golden days.

Being away from home was to me like a huge, empty park is to a excited dog. My first recollections of school life were when I was at junior school. Porchester Junior school was only about ten minutes walk away from our house. There was a small hill to climb if you took the most direct route, or it would take you about 5 minutes more if you avoided the hill. It's funny as look back now. My elder sister and I both left at the same time, and of course, we both left from the same location. I cannot ever recall at time when we actually walked to school together! Oh, there was one occasion that I do remember us walking together, but that was because it was my first day at 'big' school, otherwise known as comprehensive school. That caused a few crossed words between my mother and my elder sister, because my mother had ordered that my sister walk with me to the new school. No big deal! What's the problem there? It would mean my sister not meeting her friends at the normal time and would also mean that her friends would probably take the piss out of her for having to 'baby sit' me. My elder sister is two years older than me-ha! So to clarify, she was always two years above and ahead of me. So we would see each other at junior and comprehensive, which usually meant a very passing acquaintance.

School children tended to stick to their own flock. I mean first years would only ever hang around with first years, second years with second years etc. So even at junior school, if my sister totally blanked me, I really didn't care. It was expected. It was a crazy routine though, because by the time we were both eating our dinner, she became my sister and I became her annoying little brother. The point is we'd acknowledge each. We'd talk and argue and probably fight, causing my mother to yell at us and then send us to our rooms, but at least we didn't ignore each other.

As I remember thoughts of junior school, I always recall that it was a time in my life that I would love to go back to. I wont go into detail about the conflict that my bed-wetting caused. I think that's why I loved junior school so much; because it got me out of the house and literally elevated my to a new level. I was a different person altogether. I don't want to exaggerate or mislead. I wasn't a mute at home. It wasn't like I dare not say anything, so instead slink away and play in my own world with my pretend friends Zek and Bob. I don't want to appear sarcastic either. When I was at junior school, I wasn't under the shadow of my father.

I was a really popular kid at junior school. I rarely compliment myself or claim any aspect of my life as anything other than dour, but I had a lot of friends and I was apart of the upper echelons of the hierarchy. Even now, as I write down these thoughts, my mind is insisting that I am under a delusional episode. I used to go home for my lunch in the afternoons, on most occasions. This was a real shame because, despite what is said about school dinners, whenever I was lucky enough to have them, I used to absolutely adore them! One major bonus about having lunch at school was that you could wolf it down in a couple minutes, walk slowly away from the table, giving the teachers the impression that you were going for a leisurely stroll outside and once out of view of the teachers, you'd bomb into the play ground, screaming and shouting.

Another of having lunch at school was the 'concrete' pudding. I still, to this day, don't know what the hell it consisted of but it was lovely. You'd drown it in custard and get it down your neck as fast as possible because the clock was ticking and there was still plenty of time to dart into the playground and join your mates. Custard at junior school always fascinated me. It was called custard and it was yellow and I suppose it tasted like custard, if you closed your eyes and imagined it was custard. What interested me was it always had the consistency of water. It was thin. It was like an optical illusion!

Junior school was always the stepping-stone to comprehensive school. My attitude was always to have as much fun as I could whilst at junior school, then worry about learning and understanding what I was being taught, when I arrived at comprehensive school. I know this is not the right kind of attitude to have. I didn't ever want to go to the 'big' school. I think it was because I had made my mark at junior school. I was one of the top fighters and a lad you'd respect and not want to get on the wrong side of. Crazy I know, but as I write these words, my chest is thrust forward and I'm nodding my head in agreement.

I liked, no, loved my role at junior school. I believe a great deal of my fondness is because I was actually allowed to be me. I wasn't looked down on or feeling that I was tiptoeing on the edge of the precipice. The one where I was only a word or a sentence away from being shouted at or worse: being called useless. Of course, nobody knew that I had those problems. Looking back, I have a great deal of admiration for myself at that age. Again, that's not too easy for me to admit. I didn't take my problems to school-not junior school anyway. I think I'd come to realise that by the end of the afternoon, by about 4 o'clock, I'd be at home and as soon as I walked through the door, I'd became a different person.

I enjoyed junior school because I made the most of my freedom. Education wasn't a huge issue at the time. Sure, we were there to learn and understand, but most importantly, for others like myself who found reading, writing and spelling hard. Kids like me who found that they were constantly having to battle with the fundamentals of reading, writing and arithmetic, understood that there was a safety net attached to the years at junior school. A very important safety net - there were no exams!

I remember that I really didn't want to go home for my lunch. I do feel a little guilty now, but sometimes, when I was about to leave to go back to school, I'd look in the closet in the hall, where all the coats were hanging up. That was where the coats were supposed to be hanging up; that was where my mother liked them to be. If a coat was flung over the back of one of the chairs in the dining room or slung over the back of the sofa, the culprit was in for some serious nagging. Though I did get the blame for a lot of things that was never something that I was known to be responsible for. So, before I set back off to school, I'd slip into the closet and go through the pockets of my dad's jackets and coats. He usually had loads of loose change and like most people, he never counted it. I wasn't so stupid that I emptied the pockets! I might well go back the next day and raid the same pocket!

Later, when I was working in North Wales, a good friend of mine told me a similar story. He told me he was only a young lad at the time, still living at home. He was sharing a room with his cousin who was in his late teens or early twenties. This cousin used to go out drinking quite a lot and when he came back in the evening he'd usually wake my friend up. Or more particularly, the change changeling around in his pockets woke him up. He told me that his cousin stopped with his family for quite a while and didn't notice that when he woke up in the morning, nearly all his change was gone. He was so drunk that he didn't know how much money he had in his pockets! With my handful of change, I'd slowly slip out of the front door. I must have been good because nobody ever suspected or accused me of anything. I simply said good-bye to my mum and ran off towards the local corner shop.

This was back in the days where the corner shop was the one clichéd by Ronnie Barker and David Jason in 'open all hours'. I remember thinking that the man who owned it needed a bigger shop. Everything was squeezed and packed into such a small space. This was a typical corner shop because on three of the four walls of the shop, were shelves, about shoulder height. These shelves, from what I can recall, were the permanent residence of plastic containers of sweets! I must have been one of the owner's best customers! It was always a toss up or conflict that was a battle wills. What should I buy? A quarter of Midget Jems or will I go for Toffee Bon Bons? If I were lucky, I'd have enough money to by a quarter of each of them. However, it was usually the case that I had to make swift job of 'nicking' the money so I could only grab a handful of coins and hope they weren't just coppers.

Once I was armed with the 'goodies', I'd scurry along the road, only take me a couple of minutes and I'd be back in school. If I were lucky, I'd just have enough time to play British bulldog, dobby or football. It was usually as dependable and reliable as Christmas falling on the 25th of December, that I'd have a bag full of sweets. I wasn't greedy. I'd offer them out willingly because I knew that if I went home with them and my mother found them on me, she want to know where I got the money from. So I had to either eat them all or give them away. I couldn't take them home with me.

My sister and I did get pocket money-sometimes. It wasn't like we had to earn any pocket money. We still had to do the housework and wash and dry the pots; generally help my mother out as best we could. Sometimes we'd do our share of the housework and get absolutely nothing for it. Whilst at other times, my dad would give me a couple of quid for pretty much nothing. It was hard to work out when we were going to get any money. Because my mother didn't trust us to do the hovering or polishing properly, my elder sister and I were only trusted to do the pots. My little sister was still only young so she couldn't be expected to do any housework..... unfortunately!

There was a time when my sister and I did do the hovering as well. Naturally we both hated it - we were kids! It was my sister's idea, and I must admit as far as scams go, it was brilliant. I can't be sure exactly when this was. It may have been at the weekends or it my have been when my youngest sister was at infants school and my mother had just started back to working fulltime. I was either still at junior school or I'd only just started at 'big' school. My sister had somehow, I've no idea how or where she got this idea from, but at the time, it was like a celestial beacon showing us in the error of our vacuuming ways. Done properly, hovering all of downstairs in our house would take about an hour, maybe a little more. The definition of "properly" included picking things up and putting them back in their rightful places and not chucking them behind the sofa or, even more cunningly, under or in-between the sofa cushions. If polishing was required, again the definition of "properly" would include actually using furniture polish and not just using a wet rag from the sink and quickly running it along all the surfaces you were expected to polish. You were supposed to spray the polish on the furniture and not spray it in the air, so when mum got home she'd smell the furniture to ensure that the right spray had been applied correctly.

The most effective con, and without doubt my favourite, was instead of hovering for about an hour, we used to get the yard brush, the type with hard bristles, and aggressively sweep against the shag pile. This gave the same effect as if it was hovered and it only took a couple of minutes! To make sure the job appeared correct visually and auromatically, we'd sprinkle a small amount of 'Shake and Vac' into the carpet so it actually smelled like it was hovered as well as looked like it was hovered. It would only take us about a quarter of an hour to do the whole of the downstairs! Mum would arrive home from work around six o'clock and we'd start to clean at about twenty to six.

Friday was always the best day of the week when I was a kid. It was the last day of the week and everything and everyone was more relaxed. Walking home from junior school Friday afternoon was the best. There was always an extra thrust of adrenaline. The energy level was at maximum even though it was late in the afternoon. My mind would be lost somewhere wondering what I was going to watch on television and wondering what the score would be when my dad took me to see Notts County, on Saturday afternoon. Fridays also meant that I could stay up late and watch television because I could have a lay in the following morning. Oddly enough, back then, when I was a lad a lay-in would be defined as getting up at maybe eight-thirty or possibly nine o'clock in the morning.

The best kids programmes were always on Saturday mornings. My elder sister and I used watch television in the front room, in our pyjamas. Another bonus about the weekend was that Saturday morning was the day my parents went shopping. The fridge would be full of cake and chocolate. I would eat as much as I could as quick as could. I always wanted to be sure I got my fair share. In fact, I always ate more than my share but never seemed to get into any trouble for it.

On the road where we lived, my elder sister and I were friends with this girl who was the same age as my sister, but light years ahead of me, because I was a whole 2 years younger. At the stage, a couple of years made all the difference. We used to go round to this girls house, which was only two doors down from ours, and read horror stories from one of her dad's books. We'd scare ourselves stupid, and the in next minute play some game or sing a song. Maybe it was the comfort of knowing the horror story or the picture was in the book and so couldn't do us any real harm.

It always, or it always seemed to be on Fridays that my dad let my sister stay up late and watch the horror movie. I'm assailed with pictures and images of Peter Cushing holding a corpses brain of Christopher Lee as Dracula. To make things even more frightening, my dad would have us watch the film with the lights off. He also made sure that we were not in contact with any of the large pillows that are so handy to hide behind when you're feeling really scared. There was a glass of pop at the ready and in chocolate that had been stored in the freezer so my dad had to saw it into pieces. Not that I want to turn what is a really good memory into something else, but I did go through a stage where I wasn't allowed to drink anything after 8:30 in the evening. And as I mentioned before, I also had to take some absolutely ineffective and awful medicine that was supposed to help me stop wetting the bed.

Before the film started my dad wanted my sister and I to prove that we were older enough to be able to watch such films. Of course we would reply something along the lines of 'sure, of course we are dad.' Not good enough for my dad. He wanted us to prove we weren't afraid of the dark: show we were mature enough to handle it. His idea of us 'proving' our 'metal' was to complete a test that he devised himself. It was up to him, which we did. He knew that we'd been looking forward to this all week, so we'd pretty much do anything! One of the tasks was to go out of the back door, in the dark. Remembering that we'd have to complete these tasks about fifteen minutes before the start of the film. The films were always on from between 10:30 p.m. and midnight. So it was very dark outside. We had to go out the back door, up the steps and then across the lawn. At the end of the lawn (which as I recall was never cut - my dad hated doing the gardening!) was my dad's shed. This was a terrifying place. It was a storage facility for all his tools and it was there before we arrived. It was old and smelly and the worse thing was that it was like a graveyard for spiders! I won't set foot in it now! There were dead spiders and cobwebs everywhere. We had to walk up to the shed in the pitch black and turn the shed light on! It was usually my sister who stuck her hand through the door and groped for the light switch. It was agonising for her and me. Once my dad, who was standing just outside the back door, saw the light, the task was complete. We moved quickly back down the lawn towards the back door with huge smiles on our faces because we'd done it!

It probably reads as cruel but we used to love it! We'd hold each other's hand every step of the way. Even when my sister was struggling frantically to find the light switch, I'd have hold of her other hand. Ironically, this bonded my sister and I really close together when we were young. It was fun. I don't know why, but it was. We both look back and laugh about it today.

The other test was to walk upstairs in the dark and walk a long the landing and outside my door, stamp three times. Then, we'd walk back downstairs and into the front room. This was perhaps considered harder because it had to be done on your own! No holding hands! I always preferred this because there were no creepy spiders involved. As we bravely battled through these tests of character, our minds were brimming with images of Dracula, blood, vampires and high, deafening screams! It makes our conquest even harder and that much more admirable. I cannot remember where my mother was during those bizarre episodes. We'd tell our school friends about them and I have no doubt that they thought our family was crazy. I always thought they're funny.

I'd say I was in my prime at junior school, which is a bit disconcerting considering I was only about 10 or 11. Another bonus about junior school was you didn't have to wear a uniform! That was all about to change. My days of a relative respected level amongst my peers was about to plummet very quickly. Comprehensive school was the next on the ladder of education. As I've already stated, learning and education was never that important to me. I was always more concerned with having fun and running around, screaming and hitting girls. It is a massive and very swift transition from junior to comprehensive level.

For starters, comprehensive school is a lot bigger, which had a consequential effect on the atmosphere of the place. There were so many people that you didn't know. It meant having to build up your profile and establishing the kind of person you were. At junior school, in our first year we were all so young, so the emphasis was on enjoyment and relaxation. The first year at 'big' school was about finding boundaries and perimeters. You had to get the right balance. If you acted too soft and looked like you were easy prey, you were going to get bullied. On the other hand, if you acted too hard, strutted and swaggered too much, you were going to be a target for the really hard kids. Image was vital. It was absolutely essential in the first year of 'big' school to sell your stock as high as possible' but not oversell. You had to be able to handle your image.

The 'big' school experience started in the summer, being dragged around the shops by my mother, trying to find the right jumper and the correct trousers and worst of all, learning how to wear a tie properly! I was used to wearing what I wanted at junior school. It was never an issue for anybody. There is a picture of me somewhere in the back garden, in my new school uniform. It's a sunny day and I'm struggling to look at the lens of the camera. I'm squinting, actually. But it is blatantly apparent by my body language that I'm about as comfortable as cat in a dog pound. It spoke volumes about my attitude towards the new school.

It was always going to be an uphill struggle. What perhaps upset me the most was that I wasn't going to be in the same classes as my best friends. Because the school was so big, the years were separated into 'houses'. There were seven houses in the school and each house had five years - first years onto fifth years. The names of the houses referred to well populated tourist attractions around Nottingham – Sherwood, Newstead, Thorsby, Wellbeck, Clumber, Wollaton and Rufford. Some of these may be spelt incorrectly - this is the first time that I've had to write them down for nearly sixteen years.

I was in Wollaton, the same house as my sister, who was in the third year when I arrived. I suppose it was natural that one house would be better than the rest. I can only define 'better' as referring to the people and characters that made up that house. Wollaton was alright. The pupils in there were okay. It was better than being in Rufford, because that was full of wimps and sissies. The best house to be in, the one that everybody else wanted to be in, was Sherwood. It even had the best house name. I mean, what could say more about Nottingham than Sherwood. A couple of good friends of mine were in there as well. These two lads were two of the toughest in my old school and because they were in the best house, I think that made life easier for them.

The first couple of years at comprehensive school were unbearable. If I was having a bad time at junior school, at least I still had my perch to look down at everybody else. As I intimated before, I was well respected in junior school and I didn't have to try too hard. I was surrounded by people that I knew and trusted and I was confident about what I did, at all times. Of course, all the teachers knew me well, that was important. So the worst kind days, the days were I wet the bed, been beaten and called names by my dad, by the time I arrived at school, I felt pretty angry and frustrated. I didn't realise that I was in such a 'privileged' position at that time. I could bully somebody or take my anger and frustration out on somebody smaller and less popular than me. When I arrived at 'big' school, all of that changed. Looking back, I wished it didn't change.

Things were bad because suddenly, or so it seemed at the time, I lost all confidence in myself. I didn't have the courage or, more importantly, the faith in myself to stand up in a crowd of relative strangers and voice my opinions as much as I used to. It was brought to my attention by my teachers in the first few years that I had problems with written and verbal communication. Add to this the fact that I was completely useless at Maths, and you can see outlines of where I was beginning to struggle.

Yes, life in those first few years was a real ball! On the face of it, home life should have improved considerably. It was roughly at this time that my dad had taken a job in the Falkland Islands. He was working on Port Stanley airport. As I recall, he was away from for nearly two years. This might have been the break I was looking for. I could wet the bed and never have to be given cold showers or be beaten again. That was the theory. Even as a kid, I put a lot of the responsibility down to my dad, so with him being away for a long time, I should have found a rapid deceleration in the amount of times I was wetting the bed.

Yet I was still doing it, even when he was away. It was a real strain on mum. She had to bring up two teenagers, one with a chronic bladder problem and the other who was starting to flirt with boys, booze and cigarettes in no particular order. My mother also had to bring up my youngest sister. I don't know why, but even with my dad not there, I still lied and hid my wet stuff. To make things worse, my relationship with my elder sister deteriorated. She really hated me at this time because I was causing more grief for my mother.

At first, when my dad was away in the Falklands, my mother used to break down and cry all the time. At first, I would feel sorry for her and try and comfort her. My mum was soft and easy to get around. Years of my dad's dominance had their effect on her. I don't mean dominance in terms of violence or aggression. It was just he was the one we'd ask questions or look to for any kind of advice. With my dad absent, my tongue had a mind of its own. I could be really nasty, replying with a cutting remark and just wait for the waterworks from my mum.

During the period of my dad being away, my elder sister and I argued ferociously and I hated her most of the time, but she was supportive to my mother. I can remember playing some strange game that consisted of chasing a girl, and when catching her, twanging her bra strap. Then, I would run as fast as I could to my friends where we would all have a good laugh! We were playing this bizarre game at school, at a place called 'tit hill'. Two hillocks or embankments that were adjacent and just happened to be shaped like a pair of malformed woman's breasts.

From the corner of my eye I could see a shape, vague though it was, I could make out it was a female shape and my sixth sense strongly advised me, which rapidly became a desperate urge, to run. I didn't know who it was, but whoever it was calling my name and there was a very unpleasant, perhaps even violent overtone to that voice. It turned out to be my sister. I couldn't believe how fast she moved. I ran up the hills and then down again. We both stopped and stared at each other. Well, I started at her apprehensively and she absolutely glared at me. I knew it had something to do with my argument with my mother that morning. From a safe distance of about twenty feet, she told me I had really upset my mum and I'd better start to realise that it was tough for her without dad. I remember this scene because it was a pivotal one. It was the first time I'd really thought about my mother's situation and predicament.

It wasn't too long after this that my mother began to change. It had the same impact as the Incredible Hulk changing from 'mild mannered' Dr. David Banner. Obviously she didn't turn green or bulge out of her clothes. My mother did, however, scream at me and chase me up the stairs. She also took a definite swipe at me, but a terrified twelve year old is very hard to catch! From that period on, my mother took no more lip off any of her kids. She had, in all honesty, become empowered. She was the one left in charge and she did a good job of it! Things had altered forever in our house from that day forward.

When my dad arrived home for good, he must have been taken back by the change in my mother. She was still the same person who didn't particularly like loud music or wasn't sure about going for driving lessons. But there was a steel and determination behind the smile and soft flesh now. A new desire to prove that she could handle herself and that she wasn't reliant on other people. She still made Sunday roast and loads of cakes, but the edge was as definite as her new confidence.

Those first few years at school also meant that my elder sister and I had to go through the indignity of relying on school meal tickets. These were given out to families who were on low income and just couldn't afford to give their kids money for the school canteen or provide the kids with lunch. Remember, at school, image is imperative. Most of the lads I hung around with had money that they were supposed to spend on good, healthy wholesome food from the canteen. In fact, they went to the local shops and bought piles of junk food! Chocolate, sweets or cakes. I know this because when my dad started to earn money and send it home, I was given money to spend on the same good, healthy wholesome food.

But for a while, I had to hand my yellow or green ticket across the counter and that would pay for my meal. The value of the ticket was worth sixty pence. What got to me was the garish, bright colours of the ticket. It was an awful feeling because whilst waiting to hand your yellow/green ticket across the counter, you would be surrounded by kids who paid 'real' money. Children at that age have no heart and no inclination of emotion. It was something you'd always get teased about. Be called a 'tramp' or some other heartless name. Kids at school can be so very, very cruel.

As well as my mother becoming empowered, due to my father's work in the Falkland Islands, she had another cunning plan. Throughout my dad's time away, he used to write letters home to all members of his family quite a lot. He always told me to try my best and help mum around the house. Throughout this tale so far, I haven't been exactly complimentary about my dad. The irony was, I really missed him. Anyway, before my dad left, he sat me and my elder sister down in the front room, and in a really serious tone, as serious as a newsreader, he told my sister and I that if we were good, and if we helped mum out at home and did our homework etc, he would give us one hundred pounds each!

It doesn't sound much today, but at the time, it was roughly 1984/5, and it was a lot of money. The promise of that money, all that money, turned out to be a curse. If we didn't behave we wouldn't get our bonus. If the house wasn't clean and pots weren't gleaming, we wouldn't get our bonus. If we were late for school or came home with a bad report, we wouldn't get our bonus. If the earth wasn't in perfect alignment with the sun, we wouldn't get our bonus? In the end, we did get our bonus of £100 pounds each, as we always would. This was back in those bygone ages when £1 notes were still in circulation. We each received one hundred £1 notes. I don't know how many times I counted mine, but I know it was a lot. Not that I didn't trust my dad! It was just to have all that money in my hands. The feeling, that warm glow of happiness and delight didn't last long because like all sensible people, my parents wanted my sister and me to place the money into a back account, whereas I wanted to spend my money like a raving lunatic!

My 'big' school experience was up and down to say the very least. It didn't start well. I lost all my confidence and faith. My dad being away for so long didn't help, but the worst thing was, and it was my worst nightmare, that my bed-wetting became public knowledge! My next-door neighbour had once seen me bring some sheets down to be washed. I panicked and assumed that he knew these were wet sheets! Of course, he had no idea they were wet. I told him, of course, swearing him to secrecy and then a few days later, because I wanted to tell my best mate before he did, I told my best mate, who a few weeks later I had an argument with and he told as many people as he could!

I was already feeling quite down and having people know my worst secret was not going to make things any better for me. There was another lad at the same school who also had a bed-wetting problem. At the time, nobody knew about my problem so I was relatively safe. Everybody teased him, except me. I didn't, but I didn't help fight his corner either. Of course, I didn't want to give myself away and the best way for me to act was by doing nothing. It was a horrible time for me. No fun at school and definitely no fun at home either. My sister came into my tutor group once and noticed I was on my own, she was concerned and asked me at home what was going on. To give her credit, she didn't patronise me. She told my mother that I needed cheering up. We went shopping together and brought me lots of cheap, cool clothes to wear.

Roughly from the second year to the fourth year I was hanging around with the idiots and troublemakers. The three lads I usually hung around with were not talking to me. Actually, they were calling me names and throwing things at me, there was no talking involved. I was tougher than all of them. I could have beaten them all up, but I'd lost loads of confidence in the first few years of 'big' school. Though it may be hard to imagine, I believe at that time that I was suffering from depression. My schoolwork was terrible, apart from English. I could write good stories and poems. Unfortunately, my English teacher couldn't read my brilliant work because my writing was, and still is, very poor! I just survived these years. I hung on and fought. Perhaps it was good practise for the future.

By the start of the fourth year, I was back with my three best mates! It was like having a girlfriend. My mates and I would split up and get back together regularly. I was very lucky with the bed-wetting being made public. Nobody took notice - nobody really cared. I still feel lucky, even to this day! My last two years at school were the best. I got my confidence back because I had a lucky escape. During my time at 'big' school I was with the scouts. I was, by far, the worst scout in our troop. In the end, because I had been there for about four years, I was made a patrol leader. I was in charge of about six, sometimes as many as twelve scouts. All of the other lads were weighed down by all their activity badges. You earned a badge for all the activities you passed, there are loads and I can't remember any of them. The only badges I had were the ones you were given when you joined scouts. It was like being surrounded by majors or Sergeants, all decorated with so many honours that you couldn't actually see their uniform!

By the time I was a fifth year, the final year of school, it was the equivalent of being the boss of the mafia. We had all the privileges and fun. Best still was the fact the first years looked younger every year! We were once in that position and now we were at the top of the tree! In the first four years of school, you had to cue up at dinner and wait. The wait would take up nearly all the dinner break and by the time you were out of the canteen, the only topic worth talking about was moaning about missing most your break waiting to get into the canteen. In the fifth year, you simply strolled passed the cues and walked straight up the stairs that led to the canteen. You didn't need to turn around to see the hate in everybody else's eyes.

Most of lunchtime was spent buying crap from the local shops. We only went to the canteen if it was raining or if we needed cheering up! Drama was one of my favourite subjects at school - in fact; it's the only qualification I left school with. It was also a skive. A lesson where you didn't have to think too much or too hard. In drama, my mind had a habit of wandering. We would sit in a circle, surrounding our teacher, and she would give us scenes to act out in groups or act out in front of the whole class. Being a young adolescent, my mind took me on the well-travelled route of girls and women and you get the drift. Naturally I would react to the stimulation in my mind. I lived in fear of having to act out a scene with an erection! I prayed that I would never have to stand up and act out a scene with my teacher. It always seemed to happen in drama! Never in a classroom where I had a table to protect me!

This was a really enjoyable time for me and it was quickly coming to an end. Exams were looming around the very short and immediate corner and it meant nothing to me. I was in the bottom of all classes, apart from English, which didn't section off pupils. I knew I had wasted important years 'digging' and 'surviving'. It must look like a cope out. It feels like one, but it is the truth. I knew I wasn't going to get any decent grades and I wasn't really that bothered about it. I was more concerned with drinking with my best mate.

My sister was about eighteen and she had started to buy me drinks in one of the local pubs. It was my money! She went to the bar for me. My years of sadness and bitterness seemed very distant at this point. It was a different lifetime and a different person. I was young, confident, arrogant and most important, happy. I was drinking regularly at the weekends and most importantly; I was drinking with my dad and my sister. It was great for me because it was perhaps the first time I could be with my dad and feel I could look him in the eye, if I stood on tiptoes, and feel like a man! I think he was proud of me at that time. I was good looking and I had the crash mat of telling my dad that I was going to college to set about correcting my education. It felt like junior school again. I was so relaxed at this point. If I was out with my sister and my best mate, we used to go to the 'chippy' after closing time, buy some chips and then slowly, in a zigzag attempt at a line, walk home. My best mate used to stay at our house on Friday or Saturday nights. His mum and dad didn't know about his drinking. My parents were very liberal. They didn't mind as long as I was honest.

I didn't have to stress of exams because I was too stupid to take them seriously. My three closest friends were all really intelligent and studied hard. I remember thinking that the exams came from nowhere! I was so busy enjoying myself as a fifth year that I honestly didn't notice that every other sane and sensible person was worrying about the up and coming exams. People like me had more and more free time because our teachers were busy helping the other pupils revise for the exams. They used to let us leave early or simply not teach us at all. In my last year at school I spent many hours bored or playing football with the rest of the dunces and idiots. There's no point in pretending that I was anything other. I did have potential at that age, but I didn't see the point in worrying about exams when I was going to go to college in the summer anyway!

Looking back at my school life, it feels to me like a microcosm, a segment of what was to come. I battled and survived. It's what I do now and it seems, it's what I did then. I had some fun, in fact lots of fun. I had a lot of problems too. I know my school life will mirror a lot of other people's. It's just that, as I look back now, when I was going through a tough patch, I simply resorted to hiding away and hoping that things would pretty much resolve themselves. It worked then because I was younger and always fell back on education. I would go to college and then to university and whatever happened in between I could cope with because I always had an education.

CHAPTER FIVE
COLLEGE AND BEYOND

My college years didn't start off as smoothly as I would of liked them to have. After manfully facing my father and telling him that my school grades were going to be crap, I assured him, with a new found confidence, that I was about to embark on a brilliant college career that would steer me towards the good ship university. I knew that my school exam marks would be crap because I didn't revise for a single one. If my master plan at school was to become a brilliant, potentially huge star of the stage and screen, then my performance at school would have been perfect.... well, nearly. My single, solitary, lonely pass came in drama! You can understand that armed with a pass in drama, a subject that was about as high profile and important to my dad as needlework, I wasn't going to be in either of my parents' good books. Especially as I was supposed to be the child with the brains. My sister left school with four or five passes, including English. Fortunately, she didn't pass maths, but then again, she was in good company. Does anybody pass maths? My elder sister was always the rebel; a definite troublemaker maker/causer. I was always the 'black sheep' of the house. Who knows? If I was more confident at 'big' school and I didn't get discovered as a 'bed-wetter' I may have been much more successful at school. I actually believe that to be the case.

Anyway, I was a relative 'good boy' at school. I never played truant and very rarely arrived late. I had a good track record for handing in all required homework and coursework assignments. I would have been top of the class if all it took to gain the passing mark was to hand in the work. I was a natural at that. The problem was content of my work was nearly always bloody awful! It was either total crap or the teachers couldn't mark my work so they gave me the lowest mark available. The fact that, unlike my sister, I never got detentions nor put on report or never was the cause for phone calls home, unlike my sister, gave my parents the wrong impression the I was some kind of boy wizard who simply oozed with potential. What was misleading is the fact that for the fist three years of my 'big' school life, there was no end of year reports. These were the thoughts of teachers concerning your work for the year. You know, the ones where they end up saying 'so and so has done well, but must try harder next year'. It didn't matter who the child was. Whether it was a dunce like me or a really clever, spotty kid who wore glasses and attended computer and chess club, the end of the report always ended the same, 'must try harder'.

I can't remember my parents attending any parents evening either. I think they trusted me enough to tell them how my schoolwork was going. Like any school kid, I simply smiled sweetly and lied my head off! The bottom line was my parents didn't know that I was feeling as low as I was and subsequently had no idea how my schoolwork was. I was genuinely confident about the future at the time in my life. I remember being at this pub, speaking to my dad and telling him I had it all planned out. I told him not to worry, I'd turn out alright. I must say, again, during this account of my life so far, I've pretty much badmouthed my dad, but he was really cool about some things. He was very calm and told me it was fine as long as I took education seriously. At this time in my life, my sister had already left school and had various jobs working in a cake shop was one of the better ones. On Saturday afternoon, she used bring home all the leftovers from the shop. The whole family waited anxiously for her to return home each Saturday for their weekly dose of sugar.

My mum and dad accepted that my elder sister wasn't going to pursue any higher education. She said she wanted money so she could go out and have fun. I think my parents respected her for that. This was an area I felt I could exploit. Maybe it was rivalry, jealousy, but only on my part. It was an opportunity for me to become the 'golden child', to have the halo shining above my head. I'm not saying it was ever shining above my elder sister's head, but because I was the infamous 'black sheep' it was a chance for me to make up some points and raise my profile within the family. That's why going to college was very much apart of my master plan to take over the world. At the end of school, life was looking really good. I can't remember what job I had, but I was earning enough to go out with my sister and dad and sometimes with my best mate. I was very relaxed because for the time being all the pressure was off. I didn't have to prove anything to anyone yet! I knew once college started that the pressure would return, but for the time being, for the immediate future, my teeth glimmered when I smiled. I wore that halo above my head.

This was a great time for me. I would wake up and be really, insanely happy with the morning because my sheets were not wet. I can't put into words, at that time in my life, what it meant for me to have stopped bed-wetting. By the time I'd left school and was thinking about what college would have me, it was only about a year and a half since I had stopped wetting the bed. It did wonders for my confidence. I was quickly developing a very serious relationship with any mirror that I came across. It was like I was, for the first time in my life, recognising myself as a person. Seeing me and what qualities I had instead of feeling sorry for myself and crying alone in my room. Seeing my reflection in a shop window would mean I'd stop and pretend to look at something, while, in fact, I'd be making sure I still looked as good as I thought I did.

Just before I left school, my best mate at the time, a lad named Stephen, who a few months later I was to fall out with and never speak to again, asked me if I wanted to go on holiday with him. He actually asked me while we were watching a porno movie at my house. It was after school so it was about four o'clock. Well, to be precise, he was watching the movie while I was looking out the window, panicking in case my little sister came home. I didn't want to explain to her what the film was about! He seemed perfectly happy with the arrangement of me keeping watch whilst he watched the film. I think we argued when I suggested we should swap! He told me about his grandma's in Cornwall and he pointed out that we could be doing the same kind of things we saw on the porno movie. This was the same lad that I used to go out drinking with, I agreed that I'd go and he told me I'd need to get some money to spend.

My granddad left my elder sister and me £1500 each! Wow, did I have plans for that money! That was without reckoning on the safe, sensible attitude of my parents. They literally forced me to put the money in the bank. Only it wasn't £1500 pounds. Of course, there were three of us. My elder sister and I were in the will when he made it, and my younger sister came along after. My granddad knew about my younger sister; he just didn't bother changing the will. That will was a real bone of contention. He left the money to my sister and me because my mother, being her generous and loving self, took care of my dad's mother when she was ill. This was rewarded with my sister and I receiving the money. It was my mother simply being herself. She didn't expect any kind of reward. Unfortunately for my little sister, she was the target for many hours of teasing. Never missing a chance to wind her up, my elder sister and I used to either blackmail her into doing our choirs or we simply we told her that she wasn't going to have any money from us. The point was the money was already in our accounts. My elder sister and I had agreed to make it all fair: £1000 pounds each. But we'd lie and tell my little sister we'd changed our minds and she couldn't have the money anymore! Worst still, we'd laugh at the same time!

I did get a few jobs before I went on holiday with my mate. The problem was, even though I promised my parents that I wouldn't touch the money, I had a bankcard and I had already drawn out about £50 pounds. It was really hard to motivate myself knowing that I had lots of money in the bank waiting for me! My mate really annoyed me because he was really intelligent and was going to get good grades in his exams. If that wasn't enough, he had the foresight to take a typewriting course in the previous summer. No, it may have been a computer course - whatever it was it annoyed me because my job was working as a shop assistant and I couldn't even do that! I hated it! It was sooooooo boring, standing around pretending to be interested in what the customer wanted! The thing I had that my mate coveted was my looks! You may think I'm writing this account in front of a full-length mirror, perhaps preening myself, but it's true - my mate was ugly and I was pretty damn good looking.

This period was just before my sister moved out to work at Butlins in Bognor Regis. She took no time in teasing me about 'losing my cherry' on holiday. Losing your virginity was absolutely huge among lads my age at the time, in fact probably at any time. The golden rule seemed to be to make the lie include on older women. The older the better.... well, sort of. We all lied to each other. It seemed all the lads in the fourth and fifth years, ages from about fourteen to sixteen had more sexual experience than our fathers or experienced porn stars. I remember my elder sister giving me a book about 'safe sex'. She told me that it would come it handy on my holiday. This was the first holiday I had ever been on without my family. It was a huge occasion in my life. There was pressure to have sex. I was, and still am, very bad with matters of sex and the opposite sex. My sister didn't even have to waste her energy on teasing me. Just a knowing smile. I hated it!

The holiday was pretty average. It didn't start off too well when it was only at the last minute that I found my best mate's mother would accompany us for the first week of our two week stay, in St Ives! I was honestly thinking along the lines of the infamous sex, drugs and rock and roll theme. In theory, we could still become 'bad asses' just as long as we told his mother where we were going and what time we'd be back! I remember we used to tell her we were going to the arcades and amusements, and at the same time we were dressed, oddly enough, in black trousers, white shirts and we both wore ties. It must have been the 'in' look at the time. On reflection, it appears we were either going for job interviews or meeting our aunties or uncles!

I ended up spending a huge wedge of the money my granddad left me. It wasn't so bad because my elder sister was doing exactly the same. There is one really poetic, poignant moment that occurred on that holiday. Even the environment and the local scenery seemed to punctuate the moment. My friend and I were walking back from the beach and he turned to me and said something along the lines of 'we should make sure we stay in touch after this holiday'. He was referring to that fact that, at that time, we had both officially left school. He was going to a nearby college and I was going further afield. I had a brilliant plan, you know, the one where I take over the world and become a 'babe magnet' involved going to college. I just hadn't decided which college I should bless with my brilliant potential. Still, I wasn't going to worry because there was still plenty of time, wasn't there?

After that holiday, I saw very little of my ex-best friend. I think we went drinking a few times together, but that was it really. When I did arrive back from Cornwall, I only had a few months before I made up my mind about what college I was going too. I found out that my best mate, who was still my best mate at that time, was going to college about thirty minutes walking distance from my house. That sounded pretty good to me. At least I'd have my best buddy to hang around with. It was the first day of the new term for schools and colleges. My little sister would be in her last year of junior school and my mother was now working full time. My little sister would stay and have lunch, ie. school dinners with concrete pudding. So my mother could now hold down full time work. In theory, it was also my first day at college. Guess what? I hadn't arranged a college to go to. All that time and I just didn't get around to it! By that Monday morning of the first day of term I was panicking. In fact, I must have been a wreck all weekend. However, I was so used to lying and concealing things that I played a perfect 'pockerface' so nobody knew anything was wrong.

I said goodbye to my mother and as far as she was concerned, I was off to embark on my brilliant career at college. As soon as my mother closed the door, I ducked passed the window at the side of the kitchen, unlocked the garage door and stealthily snuck inside the garage. This was what my 'brilliant plan' was reduced to. I desperately needed a 'cunning plan' instead so I decided to hide in the garage. I was going to wait until my mother left for work, and that was something else that I hadn't really given enough thought to. I was 'rumbled' because my mother saw me suspiciously ducking under the kitchen window. It was lucky that she did see me. I swear I would have continued the lie had she not seen me. Even at the time, I could hear the theme tune to 'Mission Impossible' playing inside my head.

Why didn't I just tell my parents that I had messed up? I'm not sure. I think it was partly because I had made such a show of steering my ship back on route. School was a disaster and I wanted to make up for it. Obviously not having a college to go to wasn't as smooth a gear change that I wanted. Still it was crazy to lie the way I did. Even at that age, I was aware that I was putting pressure upon myself to perform, for my dad's benefit. I knew that I was way down the league in terms of impressing him. I wanted to prove that I was a person with potential and all I needed was the right platform. What better conditions and environment could I possibly ask for other than a college where I wouldn't be constrained by problems with bed-wetting or any of the taint that went with it?

My mother wasn't angry with me. Perhaps she felt a little hurt that I didn't confide in her. She told me to phone up the college and ask for an interview. As simple as that! I did and I arranged to see the principle of the college the following day. I don't think my dad found out what was going on. I didn't want the embarrassment and thankfully my mother didn't want to embarrass me. It was the same college that my best mate went to. For some reason, I can't recall now, I didn't start the new term until over a week late. I was looking forward to hanging with my best mate and making new friends. Sadly for me, it turned out that my best mate had already made his new quota of friends and didn't want to keep his old ones. He never actually told me that I pissed him off by going to the same college. I can't really blame him. When I arrived I simply latched onto him and his new buddies. I thought he'd be okay with that.

What was worse, for him anyway, was that one of his mates, who he really fancied, a girl named Kate, fancied me. I was very unhappy at that time. I'd gone from loving school, and in 'big school' going out drinking and really adopting a positive outlook on life, and within months found myself without direction. Life being what it is, I can look back now and say that this was a real test for me. As I stated earlier, everything had been going so well in my life for about a year or so. I needed to be strong, now was the time to show that I had definitely overcome my hang-ups from the past and now I was a stronger person. Yet, it all went horribly wrong.

I tried. I really tried to 'tough' it out and hang on. After all, fighting and surviving was what I was good at; it was what I'd become used to. Maybe I was out of practice. I mean, I went through roughly a year and a half of absolute bliss: not wetting the bed had so many positive knock on effects that I was literally close to walking on air. I realised that my ex-best mate didn't want anything to do with me. I gritted my teeth, and did make a fight of it. I chose to do subjects in English, Maths, and Physics. I must have done some others but I can't remember what they were. Just listing those subjects is giving me the shakes. They're terrifying, especially when you're not feeling too confident. In fact, my confidence seemed to completely evaporate. I was razor sharp with confidence just months before. On holiday I was even attempting to chat girls up! I didn't have sex with any, which is what I really wanted to do. I wanted to lose my virginity and become a 'real man'. It is the first time that I can recall when I needed faith in myself. I needed the support that many people find natural. When you tell yourself that things are going to be okay. You can cope because you're a good person and you actually believe in yourself. However, I couldn't find this confidence. I didn't believe in my heart that I was going to make it work at college. All of a sudden I questioned myself and my ability; and I didn't have the answers. The only "solution" I could think of at the time, and it was a pattern that was going to be repeated time and time again in, was to close myself into my own world and wait for things to change.

As I look back at those times, I realise that I felt pretty much the way I did when I was struggling at 'big school'. This time of my life is pretty hazy. This whole chapter revolves around my college years and those years in-between which were spent at different holiday camps, or as they prefer to be called, holiday centres. I can recall going to college and having to leave because I was having problems with depression. I was roughly 17 years old. Between the ages of 17 and 21, I basically played 'hop scotch' between college work and seeing various councillors.

This was my turn to shine. My elder sister had left home by the time I was at college and I intended to make my mark in the family. Sadly, a few months after she departed, my little empire was already starting to crumble. As I mentioned, she got a job working at Butlins in Bognor Regis. Butlins was like a plague to school kids my age. It was something you didn't really want to admit to, having your holidays at Butlins. While I was embarking on my college career, my elder sister was working in Bognor as a waitress. I'll give her credit. She didn't care about the reputation of the place. She told me she wanted to get away and she wanted to earn some money. She solved two problems in one move. I felt I could work hard at college and earn my qualifications, and I could then glide towards university and become successful. The world was my oyster. I felt I could achieve anything! That was before I went to college! Even then, it was more important for me to impress my parents, especially my dad, than it was for me to be truly happy.

I learned very quickly that I had come to rely on my older sister. It was the first time that she had been away from the house for a prolonged period. I knew she would leave someday, and I thought I could cope without her. But I really missed not having her around. The feeling of missing her was soon to be marinated with feelings of jealousy. The green-eyed monster made another appearance. While I was really struggling at home and in college, my sister would write and tell me how much fun she was having! There's nothing worse than that. At the time, she didn't know how bad things were for me, but her letters, though I enjoyed learning how well she was doing, I was very jealous. When I told her so on the phone, she invited me to come and stay with her for a weekend. I can't remember why I declined, it was probably because, through depression, I'd put on a load of weight and didn't want to face the world at that moment. This was something else I was going to have to get used to. She still kept in touch, which is really special because I know that I didn't return too many of her letters. She told she had moved to a new camp (I mean centre). It was on Hayling Island, not far from Portsmouth.

At this time, I was about 18. I was going through a good patch because I was at a different college and I was really enjoying myself again. I had visions of greatness again. I envisioned owning my own empire, playing for Liverpool FC, having my own harem. The visions came at a very fast rate. I thought I could achieve anything. In that period, I would also spend more time at home, hiding and crying and waiting to hear from a 'shrink', so when I was feeling good, at peace with the world, I made the most of it!

I told my mum and dad I was going to stay with my big sister for the weekend. I write this now and I'm getting excited about going there! I don't know why but it thrills me to relive this memory. The journey from Nottingham to Hayling Island takes about five hours! It just made the build up even more frenzied. I hadn't been away, anywhere, for a couple of years and I hadn't seen my sister for quite a while. She still came home two or three times a year, but to see her on her own patch, without my parents around was going to be really special. I couldn't wait. I was really looking forward to the whole experience. I wanted to freeze time and enjoy the moment at my leisure and not let it slip through my fingers and out of my grasp. That's what happens when you really enjoy yourself. You love the experience but can't control the speed at which it passes you by. It went in a blur, that's the only regret about being happy.

My sister had told me so much about this life on holiday. centres, and I really wanted to know what all the fuss was about. Also, my sister and I could really drink when we were together. I hadn't been properly drunk for ages. I meant the sort of drunk where you end up being happy and looking to the future. Not the miserable, jealous, envious drunk where you're looking for somebody to blame for your mistakes. The journey was made all the more exciting because I could face my sister, and not have to avert my gaze, or drop my eye contact because I had something to hide or because I was ashamed. I was doing really well at college. I made some mates whom I went out with regularly and I was proud of who I was.

I loved the place and the lifestyle of camp/centre life. I was drinking as soon as I arrived. I felt really relaxed and comfortable too. That's really odd for me. I'm one of those people who have to be drunk or be very familiar with the surroundings before I let myself relax. Not wishing to toss meaningless clichés around but the staff was all one big happy family. It seemed that all the departments got on well outside of work. In work, the kitchen staff and restaurant staff hated each other, but they were best mates out of work. It seemed that everybody went out in one big group. It was such a happy place to be, I didn't want to leave! It was great seeing my sister again. We are really close now and perhaps, even closer then. She knew I was having an up and down sort of life. She wanted to see me happy. I got to meet her new boyfriend. He would be around for the next twelve to thirteen years. A lovely lad named Gary. It was even better because he was from Liverpool and supports Everton, while I'm a Liverpool supporter. From what I can recall, it was a weekend of just drinking and laughing. My sister told me she was proud of me for 'sticking' with college and trying to improve my chances by using further education. To be honest, as soon as I saw the lifestyle she was living, I'd pretty much forgotten my plan to take over the world by riding the college and university wave. I was so impressed with her lifestyle, but I didn't tell her this at the time though. Her boyfriend said the same thing to me. How it was important for me to stay at college and pass the exams. I heard them, I listened to what they were saying and I even tried to believe it. I wanted to have some fun. I think that's what I wanted more than anything else. Too many years spent feeling sorry for myself gave me a real passion to make the most of any good situation.

I was supposed to do some course work for maths while I was staying down there. Not a chance! I was too drunk and too happy to think about anything to do with college. I ended up making all the work up anyway. It didn't matter. I didn't really believe I was going to pass maths anyway and I was right. I failed, but not miserably. I didn't care. Sex (or more rightly the lack thereof) was still a weight bearing down on my shoulders. I still lied whenever my mates asked me about 'my first time'. The lie grew more and more outrageous. I think at one stage, I claimed that I had sex with nymphomaniac sisters! Anything was better than the truth! was weight training at least four times a week. I wasn't Mr Universe or the 'Incredible Hulk' but I wasn't looking too bad either.

There was a really nice looking girl from Newcastle, named Charlie. She terrified me because she was so blunt and honest it was almost painful. I really fancied her. I was using the spa in the health club and I was alone one Saturday morning. I'd only arrived on Friday evening. Charlie walked in wearing a really tight, figure hugging swimming costume. I was immediately awoken from my slumber. We got talking, or to be more precise, I got lying about myself. I was doing okay. I made her laugh and she was constantly smiling. I later learned that it was called 'flirting'. She asked me to go into the pool with her. I squirmed and wriggled, very uneasy. I wanted to, I really did. Problem was, I couldn't move. Until she was gone and out of my view and my mind, I was going to have stay where I was! I had an erection and I'm sure she knew it! I saw her later that night and again I was getting on with her really well. I was good at that bit, the talking and acting tough bit, where man beats his chest and struts around. That wasn't the problem. It was the more 'intimate' aspects that I fell and stumbled over. She asked me to go to her room and I split in two. I went very red. I suddenly found it difficult to make eye contact with her. I wanted to go with her. I wanted to have sex and be rid of this demon that stalked me. Instead of it being fun, I saw it as an assignment on 'Mission Impossible'. I was scared that I wouldn't be able to get an erection and she'd laugh and point and tell everyone. So I told this lad, whom I got on well with, to tell her I had a girlfriend back home. It ruined my night because not only did a lie, but I didn't have the guts to tell her the lie myself!

I left on the Monday and I really didn't want to leave. As soon as I arrived at the centre I was dreading the point where I would have to board the coach and head back to my life in Nottingham even though I had my mates at home and I was going out at weekends. When something has marked you indelibly and you know its impact is so strong, you can try and build a case against it, but in the end, you end up following your heart. I wanted to live the same kind of life. I wanted to have fun and go out with a big bunch of friends and work colleagues. I nearly cried on the way home. I felt so depressed. I didn't want to go back to my steady, boring, college life. The only thing that improved my mood was thinking about going back to see my sister in a few months.

The trip to see my sister definitely unhinged me. I did at the time understand that my best chance in life was to make something of my self through education. I have never been a natural at anything. I've always had to work hard to understand. I have never been the type of person who absorbs information quickly. I always had to have a second or two to go over the information in my head, which, of course meant missing important parts of the next sentence and never really, properly or absolutely understanding. I went back to Nottingham with the pretence that I was going to finish college and then, unfortunately because I knew I wouldn't have all the qualifications I needed to enter university, I would have to spend another year at college 'picking' up two a three more qualifications. Still, not to worry, I was going to make, wasn't I?

No, in fact I craved the life that my sister led. It wasn't a jealousy. I wanted to have more fun than I was currently having at home. That wasn't going to be hard! I did finish college and I really enjoyed my time there. I had a huge fall out with maths. Algebra and bloody trigonometry. It was like a really vicious and painful break-up with a girlfriend. I simply ignored anything to do maths. In fact, I sulked because some of my buddies at college were doing much better than me! I ended up with a 'b' in English language and an 'a' in English literature. I was really proud of myself. This was the first full college year that I was able to attend. The college I went to after leaving school I had to leave early because I head another attack of depression. So there was a lot of pressure for me achieve something positive this time around.

I was still living at home at this time and as far as my parents were concerned, I was going to flourish in something or other. I don't think my dad was as happy as I was about my results, though to be honest, it was such along time ago, I'm not really sure. It's just a feeling I have. Even before the end of term I had made my mind up that I wanted to work away, preferably on a holiday camp (I mean centre). What I really wanted most of all was to work on the same centre as my big sister! I didn't want to ask her because that would mean letting her know that I wasn't going to go through the college/university channel just yet. Like a true coward, I resorted to dropping hints. Claiming that because I was so young, I didn't have to go back to college just yet, I might get myself a job. In fact I may even want to work away from home. Of course, this was also true. I was only about 18 or 19. I could live a little more before deciding to commit myself to anything.

At this time I had a part-time job as a glass collector in a really posh place called the 'Queen's Moat House Hotel'. I worked on Friday and Saturday nights and I don't really need to explain what the job entailed, do I? I loved working there. I had so much fun. I was offered a job to work on the bar but, I don't why, it may have been my break up with maths, I didn't fancy having to handle money. Though what that has to do with algebra or trigonometry I'm not sure! In fact, I'm still unsure that anything in real life has to do with either of these two subjects.

I made some brilliant friends at the Queen's hotel. I didn't mind sacrificing my weekends because I was having such a laugh working there. I used to have to wear a waistcoat which my shoulders look absurdly huge. I was still weight training at that time so I knew I looked pretty good. My relationship with the mirror was growing serious. Wedding bells could not be far away! I looked good and I knew it! Problem was the fact that I could 'talk the talk' but I couldn't 'walk the walk'. I'm thrilled, even now, to recall those days. I was young and bursting with energy and enthusiasm. I was young and much less cynical. I enjoyed the good times and expected my life to be always on top of the roller coaster.

Whenever I went out, unless it was with my dad or my sister who still came home to visit every so often, it was with the staff from the Queen's hotel. I remember one Sunday night, it was usually Sunday because we all worked the Friday and Saturday, a big group of us went out and one of the female bar staff introduced me to one of her friends. I remember that she wasn't bad looking and the group of us, about six, three lads and three girls, went back to one of the girl's houses. I was merry not drunk. When we were all in town, showing off, strutting, I was pretty good. I felt relaxed. When I found out we were going back to the one of the girl's houses, I began to sober up! I felt this invisible spotlight on me. I remember thinking I was on stage in Las Vegas, and I was in the glare of a spotlight. This was the night I was gong to have sex for the first time. Ironically the prospect of me having sex ruined my night! I was too scared. I don't know why sex scared me so.

I remember we were all in the front room of the girl's house and slowly couples were leaving. The girl I was with told me it was time for bed and she took my hand. My heart was galloping away. We went upstairs and she went into the bathroom and I waited outside the door. When she was done, I went into the bathroom, locked the door, found the mirror and took a long good look at myself. I was sober enough to perform. I needed to be cool and calm. What was I going to do? I didn't fancy her, but if I could have sex with her, I believed that I would be a more complete person, like a real man. My heart skipped a beat as she knocked on the door and asked if I was okay? I thought I'd better not answer that honestly. In fact, I didn't answer at all. I was absolutely petrified. When I had to 'walk the walk' I spent nearly two hours in the bathroom hiding. I crept into her room and she was sleeping. I was so relieved. I spent the night in her bed and even kissed her goodbye in the morning. When we were walking away from the house, towards the bus stop, the lads I was with all compared stories of passion and perversion. When it was my turn, I simply winked. I felt ashamed, but glad to be out of there. I was young. Didn't I have many, many more chances in life?

One of the problems with depression is that reminiscences often become murky and grey. It becomes too easy to forget the good times and only remember the bad times. Even when I do recall happy times, I hate myself for the position that I find myself in now. I remember when my sister told me, it was the summer of 1992, that she could get me a job with her in a place called Seaton in Devon. It was what I wanted more than anything in the world. It was then accepted that I wasn't going to take over the world at that point or become a future rival for 'Bill Gates' just at that moment. Even then, I still had it firmly placed, in the back of my mind, that education was my ticket out. I had already worked on building sites and in warehouses. I knew what I didn't want. Not that there's anything wrong with building sites or working in warehouses. It's just that I thought I could do better. I was still only 19 and I had the swagger of somebody who expected things to be okay.

It feels odd to write that. The fact that I was pretty confident at that time. You see I'd forgotten that I was capable of feeling good about myself. It's odd because I had so many problems a few years before that. Only three or four years before I was really struggling in life. Yet in the summer of '92' I was very happy with my lot. Before I left to work at the holiday centre (now they're called villages!). So before I worked in Devon, all my friends from the Queen's Moat House decided that we'd go out and get really drunk. It was on a Sunday evening because, that's right, we all worked on the Friday and Saturday. We went around town. My four best mates at the Hotel - Tony, Graham, Chris and Paul. When we went out we called ourselves the 'power drinkers club'. Corny I know, but I loved my time spent with them. I was part of a group and my opinion mattered. It was valid and listened to - ignored most of the time, but at least I had friends who liked my company. This seems like such a long time ago now. That Sunday night was electric! I felt so proud and glad to be alive. I had so much to live for and look forward to! I was going to be living away from home for the first time and I was young enough to be able to view this new challenge as an 'adventure'.

I remember that Sunday that the lads I was out with ran into my sister and her mates. I was drunk and happy. My friends had come out for my last 'power drinkers club' night and it was in honour of me! I had never had that before. Still, it didn't cross my mind to stay! I was leaving on the train on Tuesday and nothing that was going to stop me! It must have been a good night because it still sticks out in my memory, which is, or seems generally overloaded with darker recollections. We all promised to stay in touch and. guess what, I never heard from any of them again! It's hard to stay in touch when I didn't write to any of them and they didn't know my new address! My mother was concerned about me going away. Of course, by that age I had seen a fair few 'shrinks' and I was becoming more and more intermit with depression - I didn't know the danger signs then. I feel a slight shiver of excitement now, thirteen years and two and a half stone heavier! I had an overwhelming feeling that I was going to really enjoy myself living away from home. I needed to do it. I know now there are some good memories and bad memories at home. It's the same for everyone. But leaving home I had a strong suspicion that I could relax and be the real me. I was going to give it a try anyway.

CHAPTER SIX
LIFE AT THE BAY

It was a Tuesday that I tagged along with my sister and her boyfriend to Nottingham train station and waited to board the train that led to my new life. I was really excited – in fact I was buzzing. I found everything amusing. Nothing could deny the smile on my face or the laughter in my heart. I remember the train was late as usual. I had to move constantly because I was really brimming with anticipation! I annoyed my sister with my constant fidgeting and movement. It's a long train journey to Seaton in Devon. I knew it was a really special and pretty momentous occasion in my life and I was going to make the most of it. The longer it took us to get there, the more adventurous and exotic my ideas became. I was so looking forward to getting there, yet at the same time, I wanted the moment of tantalising fantasy and anticipation to last. I had built the camp up into a paradise. I had never seen the place before, but that didn't matter. I was enjoying the moment, and the pleasure of being able to think with so much freedom and abandonment.

We arrived late afternoon and went straight to one of the many pubs in the village. My sister and Gary, her boyfriend, continued to tell me about the place and how utterly great it was. I was like a dog that was desperate to be set free of its lead with an incredibly energetic tail. My excitement continued to bubble as I was shown around the centre. It was (sadly it's closed now) a family-orientated centre. The beach was only about 15 mins. away on foot. There were four or five bars and two swimming pools: an indoor and outdoor. I was shown my room in the main staff corridor. This worried me. For the first time my great adventure became a little poisoned. I was going to have to share a room! I was shocked. I just assumed that I would get my own room. While I unpacked and made myself familiar with my room and the staff corridor in general, my sister and her boyfriend went to their own room, which was actually a chalet.

I was introduced to Tam, my Scottish roommate. He insisted that his name was Tam and not Tom, which everybody else insisted on calling him because they knew it would wind him up. I later learned that evening, while getting very happily drunk, that there couldn't have been a worse possible roommate than Tam. That seemed quite funny when I was drunk. My time with Tam was cut short because he decided to leave. He claimed that while walking up the three or four steps to the port cabin type structure that was the staff accommodation, that he fell UP the steps. He also sustained some nasty facial injuries. He was advised to leave. It was rumoured that he got in a skirmish while drunk and fell over while staggering home from the pub. It was good for me because I didn't like him anyway. He made the room smell and his departure gave me a room all to myself.

My job at Lyme Bay holiday centre was as a waiter. My sister and her boyfriend were both doing the same and they told me it was an easy job that you made really good tips from. My sister had volunteered to 'train me up'. She taught me how to set the tables, the quickest ways of clearing down, etc. My sister made the job glamorous and easy to fit into my fantasies of my new life. In reality I was absolutely hopeless as a waiter. I was given the record of receiving the lowest amount of tips - and this happened week in and week out until I retired and worked in the kitchen!

It sounded heaven sent: my sister teaching me the ropes. We could have laugh and make the whole process fun. She was deadly serious about teaching me. She was one of the best waitresses in the restaurant and she explained that it reflected on her how I turned out as a waiter. One of the tricks of the trade, to endear yourself to your diners, was to tell them that you hadn't been doing the job for very long. It's what all the new waiting staff did. Apparently it made people feel sorry for you and enhanced your tips at the end of the week. This period was supposed to last for a couple of weeks until you become used to the job. I was still telling people after my fifth week that it was my first day on the job! I remember that when my sister was training me, I was helping her with her station. This is the area in the restaurant where the waiter's tables are. I was supposed to observe and learn. Watch her and learn. At the end, when all the guests have eaten, it's time for all the stations to be cleaned and hovered. Again I was to help my sister and learn. She told me that her station had to be hovered. All stations need to be hovered. I nodded my head. Yes I understood that. Then she told me again. Yes I understood about the hovering. And on it went. Boy did we argue. Never work with a sibling!

The place was everything I'd dreamed it would be. I was so happy and I can honestly say that it was one of the happiest periods in my life. I wanted to feel part of a team and be listened to and make my point of view known. I made so many friends, really good, close mates. Guess how many I still keep in touch with? Sadly none. I know it's one of life's many regrets. I still had a problem with sex. The fact that I wasn't getting any probably contributed to this! I was slowly beginning to evolve into a rumbling thunder of trouble. That was the only problem for me. I felt much more confident and at ease with myself. The only real issue was the sex. Though at that age, and being so much younger, I really did feel that it couldn't be too much longer. My social life was all I wanted it to be. Although I was fumbling and stuttering my way through the restaurant, I was always the last to leave.

It's all about coordination and precision. Be organised and clean up as you're going along – what could be easier? I'm not and never have been structured or organised. In the mornings, the restaurant staff usually had a notebook to take down the orders of the guests. Again, to a normal person it is not hard to comprehend. A full breakfast you'd write one full, or as many as applicable. Bacon and eggs, you'd abbreviate to something like e/b. There are various abbreviations for the different combinations. The key, the very cornerstone is to be organised! Firstly I couldn't remember what my abbreviations were supposed to mean. Secondly, my handwriting is so poor that sometimes even I could read it! What made things worse was I used to panic. I was always in a rush because I knew I was slow. That included writing down the orders. By the time I got to the kitchen and approached the serving staff I'd look down at my tatty notebook and see meaningless scrawl. It looked like Arabic or a combination of different languages. I'd often end up giving the guest what they didn't want. It was no wonder I never got any tips!

The night times were a different matter altogether. I got pretty wound up during the service in the mornings and the evenings. The best way to unwind was to enjoy yourself and three or four nights a week, loads of staff would go out together and get drunk. I absolutely loved it. I was more relaxed because there wasn't a guest in sight. I could be myself and have fun. We would go to the local pubs and then return to the centre and drink until about 2 a.m. We had to be up by 7 a.m. to be in the restaurant for 7:30 a.m. Everybody felt ill and hung over apart from me. I don't suffer ill affects from drinking, but I was happy to be a part of the group again. Bizarre I know, but I felt like I was the same as everybody else and that was very important to me. I felt I was on a level playing field. At the end of the morning service, when all the clearing down was complete and the stations were clean, the staff, both kitchen and restaurant, would go straight to bed! You'd be back in your room for about 11 p.m. Apart from me, that is. I was still hoovering and making sure my station was clean. I would finish thirty minutes to forty-five after everybody else. The difference was I had people around me all the time. I didn't feel down or depressed because I knew I had friends and I knew I'd be out with them drinking again soon anyway. It's what I always wanted. Those times, after I left school and I couldn't work because I was suffering from depression and I was waiting to talk to a councillor, the beacon for me was to have lots of friends and have fun - to feel I belonged and that people enjoyed my company. I had what I wanted and I was very happy at the time. College was still lurking in the shadows. I knew I was having fun, but life was about progression and making the right decisions at the right time. I'd told my parents that at some point I would return to college and continue my studies.

Well by about five weeks I'd had it with being a waiter! There was no denying it. I was crap! I kept telling myself and everybody else that I was just a slow learner, that's all. I was advised to work in the kitchen because, and they were blunt, it wasn't as though I was making any tips, was it? I had loads of mates in the kitchen anyway, so it was a smooth transition. My first assignment was to work at the front of the plate wash. A thankless task if ever there was one. The waiting staff would simply dump all the plates and bowls and cutlery on a surface in front of me and I'd feed it into the machine. This job required speed and dexterity. Much more up my street. Yet, I couldn't even do this job very well! I hate all kind of sauces. Tomato and brown sauce especially. The plate wash involved having to handle the sauce smeared plates in the mornings and evenings and I'd cause a huge pile up of plates because I was always washing sauce off my hands!

After about a week of causing congestion at the plate wash, with restaurant staff having nowhere to dump there plates because I was so bloody slow, I was removed from the front of the plate wash and found myself working in the pan bash. This is where all the big pans and containers are washed and stored. On reflection, both jobs were absolutely horrible. I would not even consider working in a kitchen and going through any of that again. But again, I was pretty happy. I was working with some really good mates and most of the time I was having fun. I knew I had a group of friends who liked me for who I was.

Alas this tale also has poison in its recipe. I think it was the move to the kitchen that started me thinking about how much of a dead end type job it could be working in the kitchen. College and education were always with me. It gave me a strange kind of pride that even though I was not good at washing dishes or waiting on tables, I did have a bigger picture in my head. That, of course, was the fact that while everybody in the kitchen moaned and complained about money and general glumness of working there, I was going to do something about it: college and university and the world! It wasn't all sweetness and light; it never is. Towards the end of may stay at Lyme Bay, which was about three months, I was starting feel quite low again. I would have days, maybe hours, putting myself through the torture of wondering whether I really wanted to leave and return to college and when was the best time to do it. The fact that these deliberations with myself, always alone, were weighing so heavy on my shoulders should be a good indication that, in truth, I really didn't want to leave. It was madness because I was still only young and I could leave whenever I wanted to. I think now it was working in the kitchen. I used to go home, back to my room, absolutely stinking of everything imaginable. It was really getting me down. I couldn't lie to myself any longer about doing this for another year or so. It was college. I wanted to get started as soon as possible. Not because I was enthused about the idea of getting back on track. Rather, I wanted to get it over with. I realise how crazy this seems. I had it set in my mind that I was going to be a 'someone' in life and the only way I could influence the chances of actually succeeding was getting real qualifications.

Towards the end of my stay I was starting to feel pretty low. I remember I went out one night and got very drunk. Being drunk can be such a brilliant thing when you're happy and on top of your game. I clearly wasn't feeling too good at that moment and with that fantastic gift of 'hindsight' I believe that it was absolutely the wrong thing to do. I staggered over to my sister's chalet, either very late at night or very early in the morning and woke her up. She took me to the kitchen and bless her, I can't remember her being angry with me considering that I had just woken her up. I was crying, but the tears consisted of beer mostly. I was frustrated that I was forcing myself to leave and I still hadn't had sex with a girl. This may appear complicated but I was still of the opinion that I was three quarters a man. The problems I had earlier were affecting me then. I wasn't fully confident about myself. I think, at that point, I was beginning to lie to put on a show. It was something that I was going to get used over the next 10 years of my life. I reasoned that if I had sex I would be the complete man. I could put all my problems behind me.

It wasn't long after that I gave my notice to the head of the kitchen porters. I think it was a two weeks notice. I made to decision to leave and return to Nottingham and a life of college. It was one of the worst decisions I ever made. What I needed were people around me, friends that would drag me out of my room and force me to see the light of day. By leaving when I did, what I actually did was tear up the successful formula that I discovered early on at Lyme Bay and retuned to a life of loneliness, envy and deep, deep regret. It came as shock to my sister when I told I was leaving. I never confided in her that it was on my mind. A few people came out for my last night. I think it was early on in the week and few people had money. I was presented with a huge card, which was signed by all my friends. For years, and still now, I count the card as one of my favourite possessions.

I cried on the coach, like a man, pretending I had something in my eyes. I couldn't get it out of my mind. I had given up something I really didn't want to. I kept thinking of the friends that I was leaving behind. Also, my sister and I had become really close. We used to go to the off licence after work and she would buy lager and I would buy a small bottle of whiskey. We'd go back to her room and drink it and then go out and join everybody else.

I forced myself into believing that I had made the right choice. I was only nineteen and within a few years I'd be through university and on my way. I didn't believe it on the coach and consequently I never believed when I actually went to college. Guess what? College was a massive waste of time. I decided to enrol in a computer course. It was the process of making games that I was most interested in. My tutor told me that I would have to understand the basics of computers. I told him I wasn't interested in that basics.

I just wanted to learn about the good stuff: how to make games!

I can't remember how long I lasted at college. I remember it and I hated the place before I even enrolled on the course. Just the kind of start I needed. I made a few mates at college but I missed my other mates even more. I don't know why I didn't go back. It was possibly because when depression, and at this point I was suffering quite seriously, strikes, I stop all my usual positive activities like weight training and jogging and start to eat and eat and eat. When this happens I hide away and don't go out. It angers me now that I didn't just 'wise up' and return to Lyme Bay.

Unfortunately this period of depression lasted for the next two to three years. As before, I would try and work, find myself unable to cope and subsequently have to live on benefit while I waited to see a 'shrink'. Ironically, in this time, I didn't see a 'shrink'. I understand there are thousands of people like me in the world and I was always at the back of the cue. I'd decided to ditch college for the time being because when you go for long periods feeling like a sewer rat and eventually you find yourself being able to cope again, you can't simply forget what you've been through. In the space of about six months, I'd visited the extremes of emotion and it took a hell of a lot out of me. I went through stages where, when I was out in the public, I'd walk with my face and eyes fixed on the ground and in my head was a voice saying 'know your place, know your place'. It was literally instructing me not to make eye contact with anybody else because I wasn't worthy of the rest of the world. It takes time to recover from thinking like this.

I did spend quite a lot of time with councillors. I decided I was going to try the 'wining formula' again. I applied to for Butlins Holidays. I wanted to make friends and have fun like I did before. I wanted to find that sparkle

I had when I was at Lyme Bay. I can't remember why I simply didn't return to the same place. I think I wanted to prove that I could make as much progress working on my own. I didn't want to rely on my sister. I must have really been up for the fight because I decided I was going to try the restaurant again. There is no logical reason for me walking the tightrope of the restaurant again. In fact, it wasn't even a tightrope; it was the 'plank' because I never stood a chance of actually doing the job properly.

My destination was Minehead, ironically not very far from Lyme Bay. It was another long journey. In fact it was even longer because it was by coach. I was determined to 'make it'. I had trained extensively to look my best. This literally meant losing all the weight I'd gained and being able to look at myself in the mirror. A long way away from the lad who loved the mirror. I couldn't have made a better start. On the local bus service to Butlins in Minehead, I got talking to a couple of girls who were heading in the same direction because they also had jobs there. I got on really well with one of them. Her name was Jenny and I arranged to meet her and her friend later that evening. I had also made friends with a lad about the same age as me. He agreed to meet up at the same time, as he actually fancied Jenny's friend. I was feeling pretty good with myself by the time I was shown to my living quarters. They were grotty chalets that hadn't been upgraded. I was sharing with two lads from the restaurant.

Not to sound too smug, I was looking pretty good in the mirror. I had worked very hard in getting myself back into shape, something I always did if I was starting back to work and I'd been off, on the sick, for quite some time. The issue of sex was still as huge as ever. I still believed that if I had sex, it would solve my problem with depression. On the second night I took Jenny out, I decided to tell her that I was a virgin. I'm cringing now. I was only about twenty so it wasn't the worst piece of information to impart. She laughed and told me she didn't believe me. We were in one of the most popular staff bars and music was thumping and people were laughing; not the sort of atmosphere I was looking for. I wanted for her to tell it was okay and that she'd 'show me the way'. She thought it was a chat-up line that I had perfected! When the time came for us to be alone in her room, I was a shivering dummy. I was so nervous. I'd built the moment up to a life or death scenario so it was no good me telling myself to 'calm down'. It was another disaster. We were watching 'Alien' on her bed and though I was lying next to her, there was always a gap of about two inches dividing us. I didn't want the film to end. When the time came I fumbled and stumbled and finally fell at the final hurdle. I made my excuses and left. I felt very bad. My whole world came crashing in again. It didn't matter that I looked good, inside I was still a wreck. I started to panic. I put in a lot of time physically and mentally getting myself back in shape, I didn't want to admit defeat in my first week!

To my credit I 'bounced' back really well. I made a few good mates and I nearly had a good thing going with a chalet maid! I don't know why, but things went down hill all too quickly. Like I wrote before, when you ask really searching, probing questions of yourself, you need to provide the right answers. Real, honest, authentic answers. That's where it all fell apart for me. At that time, suicide was a real issue. Depression is so painful and so damaging that you think, and pretty logically, that if life is so bad, death must be better? I was still only young but to have your heart continually broken is hard to take. By 'broken' I mean that I had put in a lot of time and effort physically and mentally getting myself back in shape. It takes a lot of self-belief to drag yourself away from the pit and back towards life. I was asking myself 'what's the point in life'? I told myself I had to fight because that's what's life is all about.

Because I worked in the kitchen, we used to nick loads of food. There was no security so we could take what we wanted. By about the third or fourth week I had done what was beginning to become standard practice for me. I would eat far too much, and hate the person in the mirror and consequently not want to have to face the public. I still do it now. I can't help it. I hide away and hate the world. I started to miss work. I couldn't go in because I felt so awful. I couldn't see my physical ailment but I know it's there because it's always there. I told my supervisor, a really nice scouser named Kevin, that I was feeling unwell. This wasn't so bad because if he followed the letter of the law I would have to have provided a medical note and seen a doctor. He took my word for it. However, this had a lot do with the fact that he was a real 'piss head' and either turned up late for work or not at all. It wasn't long after that I phoned my parents and told them I was coming home.... again. I felt very low and wanted to get away as soon as I could. I got a ticket, I think the next day, and returned by coach. Pure agony. Long coach journeys are not so bad when you've something to look forward to at the other end. Unfortunately I was staring at a familiar wall of uncertainty. What was I going to do now?

So it was back to Nottingham and more specifically, back to hibernation in my room. It takes a lot out of you when you fall to the basement of your emotions. I just wanted hide away and read. Reading was and always will be my salvation. I can honestly say that reading has been my greatest cure for fighting depression. Eventually I'd get lost in plots, subplots and characterisation. Obviously, I wasn't going to forget whom I was and what problems I had. I had the mirror to remind me of that. Reading was like the really good friend I needed to cry to. It helped soothe me for a while anyway.

Again I was out of work and claiming benefits for several months. I'm not sure how long it was until I was 'back on my feet'. I can't remember exactly, but I would have seen a councillor and I do remember going to a day care centre and having some kind of group therapy. It didn't work. I wanted to talk to a therapist on a one on one basis; they couldn't help me so I left. It's like being lost in the wilderness. I was adrift and feeling completely helpless. I remember that some of my old friends from Lyme Bay were working in Nottingham and wanted to meet up. I was elated and panic stricken. I was beginning to heal and that usually means that I was starting get back into shape and taking more of an interest in how I looked. When I go through depression I grow a beard and put on loads of weight; it's like I become the exact opposite of the person who arrived at Lyme Bay. I didn't want to meet up with Pat, Jackie and Lisa looking like a 'sack of shit' and not even feeling as good as one. I like to do things when I'm ready, especially if it means meeting the public after I've been 'off' for a few months. I hate being in public when I feel low. I feel exposed and very vulnerable.

Nobody made a comment on the way I looked - they never do. It's far to ignorant to stare in this day and age so nobody stared or said anything regarding my appearance. I had a good night. We agreed to meet again and discuss the possibility of working on another holiday centre, on Hayling Island, the same place where my sister worked when I visited her when I was still at college. In the end, I decided to take the bait. What could go wrong? I needed to get away from home and this time working away on the centre had to work because I had some good friends around me. Pat, he worked with me in the kitchens and I got on with him really well. I felt quietly confident this time.

The place was called Mil Rythe on Hayling Island, just off Portsmouth. Again, it involved a long coach journey from Nottingham. Maybe it's because I'm just plain foolish, but I always seemed to pick Butlin destinations that were at the other end of the country.

I was travelling with Lisa, who was Pat's girlfriend. Jackie and Pat had left the week earlier. There are three Warner Holiday Villages on the Island - Lakeside, Mil Rythe and Sinah Warren. They are near each other because the Island is so small. Again I was attempting to tackle the pitfalls of the restaurant. Why? I can honestly say I have no idea. Though I did like the idea of not stinking after doing my shift. A shift in the kitchen must be the equivalent of swimming in a sewer. I think I was doing my best to recreate the situation I found myself in when I arrived at Lyme Bay. Perhaps if I could do that, I would have a reasonably stable life for a while.

As luck would have it, I was to share my room with another really strange bloke. Worse still, the rooms had bunk beds! Being diabetic I told my boss that I didn't like to have my injections in front of anybody. He sympathised and promptly gave me my own room with a double bed. Even then I doubted it would come in handy for anything other than sleeping. Again, like with most of my rollercoaster rides, things started off well. The usual kind of fare. I made friends and went out. I kept up with my training. I ran and I did weights. If I felt if I looked good, then I would have a better chance of really making a go of it. I even saw my sister a few times. I started to go through a ritual of literally telling myself that I was a good person and I could make this work for me. If I really believed then I could be happy. That's were it all starts to disintegrate. You need to genuinely have faith in yourself. It's absolutely imperative. The blueprint for the perfect person should start off with the individual having faith and believing in themselves. I didn't and I paid the price. I didn't really believe and so I had no support. The end was to come very shortly. I lasted about two or three months. I couldn't go on. I'd had enough and once again all I wanted to do was hide away again. Depressive thinking is a very destructive mind set.

The latest failure really hurt. It was all very well insulating myself at the start, telling myself that because I had some friends and my sister, it really had to work this time. The problems really started then. I didn't work, even though I had family and friends around me. My life returned to hibernation and books. I talked to more councillors and I think I started to grow cynical and bitter. It wasn't as if I wasn't trying to make things right. Some time in my 21st year, I recovered enough strength to have another crack at the 'holiday centre' lark. This time it was at Butlins World Skegness. Much closer to home and I opted for the kitchen straight away. No narrative or plot this time. I failed miserably. It was my worst experience of all and I think I have never felt lower or worse than I did when I returned home from there. By now I was of the opinion that I would fail anything that I attempted. Depression to me now is a huge, invisible wall of negativity. I simply can't see the point in living. Back then; I think I was just beginning to doubt my ability to accomplish anything.

Christmas time was becoming more and more difficult to face. It's a time of fun, anticipation and love. Good to be with a loved one, not just family, I mean somebody that you care about. I was feeling more and more isolated and stranded. The previous yuletides had been tough. From years 1991/2; 1992/3; 1993/4, I had spent Christmas at home and found the 'New Years' bit even harder. The festive time when I was 21, the same year I'd arrived home from my experience at Sgegness, was the worst yet. Having said that, the year before wasn't too great either. I went out with my dad, elder sister and her friend, Sharon. I was determined to have a good night and see the New Year in standing tall and fighting hard. Other years, I'd spend New Years Eve in my room, fighting off thoughts of suicide. It's an awful experience. I could hear the laughter and singing on the street. Television was full of happiness. I was desperately trying to avoid it. For me, New Years Eve means another year fighting off depression and bitter tears. The New Years Eve of 1993/4 I was out with family and I wanted to enjoy myself. Up until the countdown, I was fine. The nearer it got, the more I began to tense. I got very drunk because I thought if I was hammered I would somehow be protected from the deluge of sadness that I usually got. We were in a pub, surrounded by loud, happy, drunken people. When the celebrations started I ran out of the pub and sat alone on a wall, opposite the pub. Eventually, when the pub was closing, my dad and sister and Sharon approached me. They were singing and happy. They knew I found it difficult but I was okay, they'd found me. My dad asked me if I was okay and I screamed in his face and ran off down a side street. He immediately ran after me and I hid behind a wall and watched him run by, I didn't move until much later.

I have no idea why I did what I did. I think it was the thought of another year of the same emotional rollercoaster.

My dad eventually found me, an hour or so later, and drove me home. As soon as I walked in the door my mother was shouting at me. Telling me I needed help. It was concern and perhaps anger. I had worried my parents for years and now I'd done it again. My response? I started pounded my head against the wall. Why? I've no idea. My parents were worried about me and called out the paramedics. It was decided that I should be taken to the local mental hospital, which ironically, was right next to the pub that I was drinking in earlier. I was admitted early on 1st January 1994. That was my welcome to the New Year! I stayed in hospital for 6 days. My family visited me a couple of times. It was arranged for me to see somebody, a councillor. It didn't do any good, obviously. The rest of the year wasn't any different from the previous one. I was just trying to stay sane and running after the hope that this year would be the one where I found some kind of balance.

I was on my own for New Years Eve, alone in the house, getting drunk and dancing to music. All sane and normal people were out having fun. Again, I was determined to put up a fight. It's very sad for me now, to reflect on the fact that I was getting drunk on my own, pretending to have fun to be able to face the New Year. Same old story really. As 12 midnight approached and then passed, I wanted to feel anaesthetised from the impeding doom. I'd had enough. I had nothing to look forward to and scant memories to fall back on. The years of failure put so much pressure on me, I wanted to die. Or should I say, I didn't want to live. If I could sleep forever and never have to face the bitter cold of reality that would be the perfect answer. Depression had taken over. I spend a lot of time sleeping - not because I'm lazy or tired. Sleeping is the only time when I have no control over my thoughts. My consciousness is free to roam and wander, to soar and glide, to go wherever it wants to.

I took eighty cocodomal tablets. They are strong painkillers. I scribbled a note to my parents. It basically said I was sorry. I felt guilty about the pain I had caused, and would cause. You have to have empathy. I was living through hell. I didn't want to have to wake up and stare at another grey, rain sodden sky. People who suffer from depression can only suffer for so long. I couldn't bare the thought of waking up again. My parents came home not long after and I stumbled down stairs hugged them both and told them that I loved them. A few hours earlier, I had spoken to my little sister on the phone. She was out at a party, and she came home and told my parents that something was wrong. I wouldn't tell anybody what I had taken and I was rushed to hospital and my body wash flushed intravenously. The paramedics had found the box to the tablets. Well, the 'black sheep' had struck again! I had made my mother sick with worry and I was driving my family crazy. It was the only time I had ever really intended to kill myself. I didn't feel ashamed, just dazed and confused. Now what was I going to do?

CHAPTER SEVEN
BODELWYDDAN CASTLE

So 1995 didn't start off too well. A suicide attempt at the end of the year is not the best way to start a new year. I knew I had hurt my parents and I didn't ever think I could make it up to them. How could I? The year was nothing special. More frustration and good old-fashioned green-eyed envy were brimming and bubbling behind my false smile. More pointless employment working at employment agencies. More laughing and joking at work, but it was an act I had perfected. I knew I had to try and fit in. Walking around with a long face and sorrow filled eyes does not make life any easier at work. So I endured and struggled on. Early on that year, my elder sister told the whole family she was pregnant. I was thrilled for her but it made me pathetic existence seem even more blunt and pointless. The happiness her news had brought in the house was incredible. My mum, especially, was chirping away like a proud mother. My dad is a typical man. Very proud, just careful not to lose his image over it. My little sister was really chuffed too. Not being selfish, it made my life much harder.

As I have already written earlier on, the pregnancy developed complications and the baby, Jake Everton, was born prematurely. While my sister was in hospital, in north Wales, my parents went to see her. In fact, my grandma and granddad also went. I didn't. I didn't feel like it. Nothing was said about my decision. It was expected that I would let somebody down - I always do! The baby died, of course, and it was a hard time. I wrote a letter to my sister, before the problems occurred with Jake, but while my sister was expecting. I told her how low I was feeling and that I was pleased she was happy with life and she was pregnant. I told her I didn't care if her baby lived or died. That it would make no difference. I never meant any harm by the letter. Obviously I wasn't to know that she was going to lose her child. I deeply regret writing it now. To her immense credit, I don't think she has ever held it against me.

I went to Jake's funeral and it was the first time that I saw Bodelwyddan Castle. It is located in Denbighshire, North Wales, about five miles away from Rhyl. My sister later told me that she wanted me at the funeral to see what damage it causes, to witness the tears and sorrow for myself. Before I left, with my mother, my sister said that she would try and get me a job up there. I thanked her and left it at that. I didn't expect to hear about the subject again. About a month and a half later, I received a phone call from the head chef in the kitchen. He offered me a job. I think that I had sent an application form earlier. I was shocked and very excited. He asked me if I knew how much money I would make a week? I knew that when you 'live in', which means you stay in accommodation provided for by the hotel, you have heating, lighting, food bills etc. to take into account. I said something like 'one hundred and fifty pounds.' He paused and replied that I would only make that amount of money if I 'lived off' the hotel. I felt stupid because I already knew that. I wanted to make a good impression, that's all. It was decided. I would start work on 8th December in the kitchens. I thanked him and punched the air in delight. I was going on another adventure! Oddly enough, I had a really good feeling about the place. I'd only seen it once, true, but my reaction on hearing that I was going to be working there was an indication that I 'believed' in this place.

My sister later phoned me and we arranged that she would pick me up from the train station in Rhyl. The phone call by the head chef must have only been about a week before I actually left. To give my parents immense credit, and they deserve it after all the harm I have caused them, they were very honest with me from the start. They didn't want me to go. Not through worry or concern for me, well, I don't think so anyway. They were much more concerned with the affect my presence may have on my sister. I had proved a failure time and time again and there was genuine concern that I would ruin all the good my sister had created for herself. They were right. My sister was taking a huge chance in taking me under her wing. She knew the pile of crap I had created for myself over the years. Still, she believed in me. She had more faith in me than I had in myself. I can remember her telling me she didn't think there would be a problem. I was really excited at the thought of going. It was like I had suddenly been animated with the brightest, most garish colours. I really wanted to go. To 'really' want to do anything at that stage was a major bonus for me.

I remember sitting our front room, not the 'posh' one, and telling my parents I wanted to go. I promised them I wouldn't do anything to harm my sister's hard work there. It was, at the time, an empty promise. I was in no position to promise anybody anything, and we all knew it. They told me they didn't think it was a good idea, but there was nothing they could do. I left on 7th December, 1995 and at the time it was the best decision I had ever made. I was, as always, determined to make it work 'this time'. Before I left to work on the other holiday centres, I got myself into good shape - and look what good it did me! It just gave me a little boost. To know that I looked good was at least a step in the right direction.

On this occasion, I didn't feel good about the way I looked. I hadn't had long enough to slim down and feel comfortable this time. I travelled to Rhyl on the train and had this conversation with myself, whilst looking at my reflection in the mirror. I was going to have to try harder! As I reflect now, something very strange did happen to me in this time. I know it was the same year that kicked off by trying to kill myself and for months after the event, I was stumbling my way through life - as always. Then this chance, this opportunity to make things right came along. Not simply a job, but a chance to be happy again and steady the ship. Looking at my reflection in the mirror, I felt a twinge, a buzz of adrenaline within in me. It wasn't exactly surging or coursing through my veins, but it was there. No doubt my sister's faith in me had a very big impact. Just to hear those words at a time when life meant even less to me was a very important.

I was really nervous because I was going to be the new boy in the kitchen and I had the pressure of knowing I couldn't afford to get things wrong this time - more for my sister's sake than my own. What a great time to be offered a job. It was just before Christmas. If all things went well, at least this time I'd have a half decent Christmas. When I arrived, I was given a brief look around and then shown my room. It was a really big room and this time I knew I was going to have to share. It was no shock and I wasn't really that fussed this time. The accommodation for the live in staff was separated into two areas. The area that I was to live in was known as TVI. I never knew what it stood for.

The other area was for the management. It was a couple of paddocks opposite the outside bowls rink. Like Lyme Bay, the corridor was long and had rooms on either side of it. At one end of the corridor were stairs that led to and from the building, at the other end was a window with a large sill that you could sit on. The view from this window is absolutely breathtaking. The castle is in a rural area and is surrounded by pastures and fields. This window gives a view of the fields and land - a real 'patchwork quilt' effect.

The hotel, a Warner Holidays hotel, catered for adults. At that time, Warner had not long taken over Butlins, so it was a large company I had gotten myself involved in. There was a leisure suite, with a small pool and even smaller gym and a couple of tennis courts, huge indoors bowling rink and a smaller outdoor one. I was really impressed with what I'd seen so far. I was shown the kitchen and stared at by the staff. I was introduced to the head chef and the second chef. That night I went out to one of the bars that was situated in the hotel itself. There are three bars on the centre, plus a bistro and a bar in the leisure suite. From the first night I went out, which was the day I arrived, I knew that I would love the place and that things would work out. There were a lot of staff that were out that night and I was really relaxed and enjoying myself. I was with my sister and Gary, her boyfriend. I was actually looking forward to working the following day!

Remember how I seem to attract oddballs as roommates? Well, the 'twilight zone' phenomenon struck again! I was sharing with a guy named Matt, who was also working in the kitchen. There was a joke going around about him as soon as I arrived. He claimed he was a certain level of chef, an advanced stage. I'm unsure exactly what it was, but the joke was, in fact, he was just a normal salad chef, or something along those lines. People used to stick signs on him, which said 'I'm a salad chef or I'm a kitchen porter'.

He was well known for making up stories and lies. The first week I was there, while we were both in our room, he came up to me and very seriously told me that if I wanted to hide some hard drugs in the room, the best place to hide them was under the drawers. I had my sock drawer open at the time, so I wasn't sure if he meant hide the seriously hard drugs under my sock drawer or would any old drawer do?

After I'd been there for about three weeks or so, everybody had a couple of days off before the really busy holiday period. Rarely during the year did the kitchen or restaurant open for service in the afternoons. Lunch was very rare. That is, until the festive period. Kitchen staff and restaurant staff had to work three shifts: breakfast, which began at 8:30 until 9:30. Taking into consideration that it takes a long time to clean down and then set the station up for lunch. Many of the restaurant staff was finishing their morning shift after 11 o'clock. At around 12:30, lunch started and they were not finished from that until around 2 o'clock in the afternoon. At 5 o'clock they were back in again for the evening meal that began at 6 o'clock. This was the schedule was hell to have to work. They did make very good tips though, that is if they were any good. It's highly improbable that anybody was as bad as me. I'm strangely proud of that fact. So the little break before the festive period was very important. I was very happy because as soon as I arrived I felt very secure. Odd, I know, because I was new to the place, but I tell you, Bodelwyddan is a magical place. I had continued to train and work out while I was there and I had lost a lot of weight. I felt fantastic, honestly, the best I have ever felt. I was swaggering and I'm sure I developed a walk the same as 'John Wayne'. I felt reborn and revitalised. I had faith in myself and I had so much to live for. A very good indication of how I felt was the fact that I was spending some of my wages on new clothes! I hadn't bothered with new clothes for years because I very rarely went anywhere. Now I wanted to buy new clothes to show off my new found confidence.

My sister had just started working in the shop at the hotel. She was an excellent shop manager. She won the highly coveted title 'shop manager of the year' in either 1996 or 1997. She would have won it the following year but they decided it wasn't a good idea to let her win in consecutive years! Staff, including high profile managers, used to go into the shop so they could have a coffee and slag the rest of place off with her. She used to have a little kettle and cups at the ready. I finished my shift in the kitchen early in the afternoon. The drive back to Nottingham takes around three hours so we'd be back home around three or four o'clock. I couldn't wait to go home. Don't get me wrong. It was nothing to do with missing home. I missed my mum and dad and little sister, of course. I wanted to go home to strut my stuff! I hadn't let anybody down this time and I honestly believed that I wouldn't. I lived in a corridor of young, funny, energetic people. I was one of them; I was living and I was apart of life again. People listened when I spoke and I was making real friends again. I was alive!

So the return home for me was a chance to look my parents in the eye, hold their eye contact and tell them that I hadn't let anybody down. I was incredibly proud of myself at that period. I think it is the only time that I have really had any respect for myself. It was like I was patting myself on the back. I had been through a very bad stage and now, it really did look, and more importantly, it felt, like I was coming out the other side. I wanted to go home and feel an equal part of the family. I wanted to be able to share in conversations and add my viewpoint. More importantly, I wanted to feel that I had a point that was worth listening to. I can understand their concern for my sister's welfare. As I inferred earlier, and the facts back this up, my history and track record were not very good. I wanted to let them know that my sister was right to have faith in me. She was right and they were wrong. She had faith in me even when I had lost all confidence in myself.

Going home gave me a chance to grab some more of my things and load them in my sister's car. When I left to work at Bod (I'll refer to Bodelwyddan as Bod - it's easier) But I was in a hurry. So I didn't take as much as I wanted. So we spent a few days at home and I think I managed to heal a few rifts that had developed between my parents and I. I was really looking forward to going back. There was going to be a Christmas party -ca big one. All the staff from the hotel would be there, and that's a lot of staff. Even better was the price of beer. A pound a pint! I can't tell when the last time I had been invited to a Christmas party. I knew that I was going to have fun that year. It wasn't a case of forcing myself to have fun. I was simply going to go out with my friends and relax, and let enjoyment find me and not force myself to get drunk in the hope that I would find enjoyment and fun.

That year, 1995, was also the first time that I really looked forward to a New Years Eve. I was like that kid who arrived at Lyme Bay, only more excited because I lived through a suicide attempt and I was about to welcome in the next New Year. Even more bizarre was the fact that I was given some really pathetic jobs in the kitchen. Front of the plate wash and working in the pan bash. Still, it didn't matter too much because I was happy with who I was. I was really content to look in the mirror and feel comfortable with what I saw.

Things continued to improve into the New Year. I was promoted in the kitchen to working in the stillroom. This is where all the restaurant staff collect the teas coffees and fruit juices. I had to make up plates of cheese and biscuits and become adept at learning how to hold 3 hot tea pots or coffee pots without burning myself, screaming and then swearing. Of course, it took me a while! It was a definite improvement on the other jobs I had. My roommate, Matt, left shortly after the January. For a while I had my own room, but spare rooms were at a premium so it wasn't long before I was sharing again. I used the gym more than any other member of staff. I was proud of that. I still had my bouts of depression. It never completely abandoned me. I got myself a girlfriend, which I'll explain in more detail in the next chapter. There you have it. The best indication yet that I was normal and I could live a normal life.

One problem did develop though. My new roommate, who name was also Paul, was gay. I am not and have never been homophobic, but this was a tricky situation. He was definitely gay. Everybody knew he was gay. He never actually admitted he was gay, but he was. My girlfriend at the time suggested that to make things a little easier, on our day off, I go into Chester with Paul and casually let him know that I wasn't bothered about his sexuality. He was good friends with her and apparently confided that he thought there was a bit of an atmosphere between us. No problem. I wanted to please her so I told her I'd do that - how hard could it be? Well, it turned out to be very difficult. He knew I was going to tell him but that made it no easier for me. We spent 4 hours walking around Chester, shopping or drinking coffee, but I couldn't find the right opportunity to bring the subject up. He didn't even admit to me that he was gay and I was telling him that I knew he was gay, and it didn't matter! In the end, I couldn't tell him. We were sitting in our room, him on his bed and me on mine, and I suddenly blurted out, sounding quite drunk, that I knew he was gay and it didn't bother me. He laughed and said alright. That was it!

By the middle of 1996, I was very comfortable in my new world. I'd been there for less than a year and I treated the place like my home away from home. That was the year of the football European Championships in England. England got to the semi-finals and were beaten on penalties by Germany. Some of the games, especially England against Scotland and England against Spain, I watched with a large group of friends. It was something I always wanted to do, watching a football tournament with a group of friends. In the bad old days, it something that I always dreamed about. It was further proof that I was on the mend. I was a new person, living an ordinary life.

I was offered a job in the leisure suite. Because I was about the only member of staff who ever used the gym, it was thought that I would be the ideal candidate for the job. It was a hectic time. I was going out a lot with my new friends. I had a really good relationship with my girlfriend. I was popular in the kitchen, but the thought of working in the leisure suite, full time, was a real bonus. It was decided I would do a few shifts in the leisure suite in my own time, and sometimes work there on my day off. My boss in the kitchen, Roger, wasn't too happy about me leaving to work in the leisure department. I don't know why, but it was a fact that I preferred his staff to leave, other than work for other departments in the same centre. Also around this time, my girlfriend and I were discussing the possibility of moving from North Wales to Berkshire, England. Warner had centres all over the place and they were going to open a new centre a couple of miles outside Hungerford. The new centre was called Littlecote House Hotel and it was in a really posh part of England! It was a really big decision, especially for me. I was happy where I was. I was about to move into the leisure department and I had a lot of friends in Wales. My girlfriend, however, really wanted to go. A lot of people who worked with us at Bod where going to work at this new hotel, so it seemed like a good opportunity. The 'big move' to the new hotel didn't take place until April 1997. I felt good to be in demand. My new boss in the leisure suite didn't want me to go and my girlfriend really wanted me to go. Can you imagine? The lad who less than a year before didn't have any friends and absolutely no hope of any kind! It's amazing how thinks can go from bad to good, and from good to bad, so quickly.

I had been further boosted by the fact that I was now working in a job that I really enjoyed and a job where I got to wear a really cool uniform! Well, it wasn't that great. Blue shorts and a white top. But I did get to show my legs off! I had two love affairs at this point: one with my girlfriend and the other with any mirror that would hold my reflection! In order to become a proper, legal lifeguard, I had pass an extensive four day training programme. It dealt with life saving techniques, fitness and first aid. Though I liked the job because it was clean and fun and I didn't stink at the end of my shift, the problem was with responsibility. What I feared about being a lifeguard was that somebody would need my help, be it resuscitation or a situation where I had to take control. Unfortunately, that was part of my job description: save lives and be organised! Fortunately, nothing major nor minor ever happened when I was on duty.

By June, I was at a new hotel but I had the comfort of being with a girl I loved and some of my good friends had also made the journey South to work at the new hotel. The leisure suite was much bigger and had more facilities. When we arrived, Jinny and I had a really poor room in the main staff block. It was a long fragile building that moved if two people spoke at the same time. It was a small room and a huge disappointment. We were promised big rooms and a staff bar to hang out in. Crap rooms and no staff bar, which meant staff would have to pay around £2.40 a pint, same as the guests. Not so great when the wage wasn't brilliant! I left a week after my girlfriend because they hadn't found a replacement for me in Bod. What made matters worse was Jinny's best friend, Donna, had a bigger and better room than we had. Her boyfriend, Tony was to become a supervisor in the restaurant. That really annoyed us. At Littlecote House, it was my girlfriend who was much more at home. She settled in well and made a lot of new friends. I made new friends too, but I missed Wales. Things weren't as good as before but at least I was not suffering from depression so things weren't so bad. I thought I had finally beaten depression. I had friends and a girl I loved and I had a pretty good life. But, not long after we arrived at Littlecote House, I felt I had made a mistake leaving Bod.

In the summer of 1997, Jinny and I went to Crete for a week's holiday. It was a big deal for me. Holiday with a girl, sharing the same room and the same bed - well nearly. We had to push two single beds together because somebody in the booking office cocked up. Ever since we arrived at the new hotel, Littlecote, Jinny and I were drifting apart. She was really happy there and I.wasn't entirely happy there. By the time we went on holiday together, we were getting tired of each other. When you have arguments on holiday, a lot of them, you know you haven't got long left.

Soon after we returned from holiday we split up - bet you didn't see that one coming! I took it very bad. I was struggling to keep on top of depressive thoughts. Though I pretty much had what I wanted, i.e. friends, a social life, etc. it wasn't enough. I was unhappy where I was and my relationship with Jinny was going downhill. It comes back to being in a place that I wasn't comfortable with. It was really getting to me. So I didn't handle the split very well! Jinny and I agreed to be friends. We also agreed not to see anybody else on the centre. She had decided that she was going to leave anyway and I was feeling the same.

I phoned my sister up and she came galloping to my rescue once again. She took a few days off and came to see me. I was very relieved she was there. I was having problems with the assistant manager of the hotel. He was gay and one night, he and large group from the hotel all went out together. This was about a month before Jinny and I split. He got very drunk and I saw him staring at me. I thought it was because he was drunk and happy. I left early and went back to our room. I washed and went to bed. There was a knock at the door and I wrapped the quilt around the lower half of my body and answered the door. It was the assistant manager. I stood there looking at him and to be honest I didn't know what he wanted. He propositioned me, at the entrance to our room. I told him I wasn't gay, that I had a girlfriend and he was drunk. I told him to get some sleep. It scared me! How do you handle something like that? He was my manager. I had to be careful how I reacted and what I said. One night when my sister was down, a few of us went out and went out, the assistant manager included, and he started staring at me again. I didn't want to confront the guy. That's the bottom line. It was a horrible situation that needed to be dealt with and I didn't want to deal with it.

I told my sister about this 'problem'. She saw for herself that the guy was intimidating me. That's what it was. He was an assistant manager and I was an employee. My sister got angry. She was a drunk and took me by the hand, walked up to the assistant manager and made out that our family, in particular my sister and I, were very close. I think she touched my knee at the same time, to punctuate the point. The guy was too drunk to be shocked by the implication. It was funny. My sister was drunk and trying to imply that I wasn't gay at all. I was, however, involved in a 'dark and seedy' incestuous relationship with my eldest sister! At the time it was scary. Now, it's just funny. My manager was gay also. He got wind of the attention I was getting off the assistant manager and told him to 'cool it.' He did and that was the end of that.

Not long after my sister returned to Wales, I handed in my notice and decided I was going to return to Wales as well. I was offered my old job back and it made perfect sense. It wasn't hard saying my goodbyes. It didn't take too long either! It was very hard bidding farewell to Jinny, though. We had remained mates and in our two years together we had become pretty close. I didn't think the split up would affect as much as it did. When it came to saying goodbye, I knew it would be difficult. I wanted to be strong and use my swagger and beat my chest like an alpha male. When it came to it I burst into tears like a big girl! So did she, so it wasn't so bad.

The evening I arrived home, back in Bodelwyddan, there was a hat party taking place in the paddocks. I didn't want to go but somebody thrust a crap orange, plastic hat in my hand and I went along anyway. I had a good time. Though I felt crap inside, I was also really glad that I'd returned to Wales. The staff were brilliant. I mean, a hat party! I was living back up on TVI, the main staff accommodation. It was a lot different from when I was there. I don't mean that there were any physical changes. Rather, the people were different. It was so quiet. All the doors were locked or shut and there was hardly a sound. I had hoped for all my old mates being there - like the old times. I suppose I wanted to just 'fit' back into the old routine. So that was a big disappointment. I naturally assumed that there would be new faces, but not so many! There was hardly anyone that I recognised. I was sharing my room with a guy from the kitchen. I think his name was Pat, and compared to some of the other people who I had the good fortune to share a room with, he was pretty normal. He was never in the room far a start! It was over a week before I first met him! One thing that I was on top of was my weight. Usually, when I hit the depressive wall, I pile on the pounds and this exacerbates the problems. I went running most days and if not days, them I ran at night. It was a tough, traumatic time for me. Breaking up with a loved one was always going to be an uphill struggle. I felt bad, but it was nowhere near anything like a real depression. I still had friends and I had my sister near. I knew I still had faith in myself too. I had come a long way and had improved as a person.

The supervisor who phoned me up and offered me my old job back left to be a manager in a nearby council leisure centre. My boss, Liz, panicked a little. She needed to replace the guy quickly. I was promptly promoted and made the new supervisor of the leisure suite. That was pretty good. Within a month of returning to Bod, I had been promoted to manager. I was really proud of myself. I'd gone through a horrible crisis in self-confidence and I'd come bursting through the other side! I was still in touch with Jinny at this time. I phoned her at her home and told her the news, though she didn't sound as excited as I was about it. I think that was the last time I ever spoke to her. Even better was the fact that I'd been given better hours and better still, I'd get more dosh! The downside was that I was told that I would be sent away on courses. These were course in management training for archery; fencing and a pool plant room course. This is where people in leisure centres learn all about pool filters and chlorine and other chemicals that are put into the pool. I really didn't want to do these courses. I was especially worried about the pool plant room course. I was happy to accept the improved contract and better working hours. I just didn't want to go away and do these courses. Still, you can't always have it your own way.

I think the reason why I was reluctant to go away on any of the courses was because my confidence had taken a bit of a pounding. I wasn't happy in Littlecote and I had fallen out of love with my girlfriend. It all added up to making me feel less secure about myself and about what I was capable of achieving. I don't care what anybody says, promotion, which involves a little gold badge with the word 'supervisor' on it, means a change of attitude. I was like the queen. Extremely aloof, making sure that everything was clean and everybody was working. I thought I was doing pretty well in my new role until one the girls behind the bar, Snappy, told me I was acting like a knob head! I had to agree with her. After that, I was back to doing my job and having a laugh.

The courses turned out to be absolutely brilliant for me. I had a really good time on every one of them. I think another aspect of fear was the fact that at the end of each course there was usually some kind of test. With the archery course we had to prove we could instruct, in front of the examiner. Same on the fencing course and there was a pretty hard test at the end of the plant room course as well. I'd gotten my feet back on the ground when I returned to Wales. I'd been through a shaky time and I had recovered. I think the courses, and more specifically, the tests at the end of them, required me to be strong and have that level of faith in myself. I didn't know if I believed in myself and the real fear was what if I failed. I was really frightened that failure would mean my mind completely turning against me and bringing down the shutters so I couldn't see the light. Failure at that point would have been unbearable.

During this period, my sister and I travelled back home to Nottingham to see our parents. I was still very proud when I went home. I was still the lad that my parents thought would ruin my sister's happiness if I worked with her again. It did motivate me, though, to prove that I was a success and that I had coped was still really important to me. On one particular visit home, our whole family went to the local pub. As we left the last pub, my sisters' and mum got in a taxi and I decided that I'd walk home with my dad.

It was all uphill but my dad was and still is very fit. Like all things that inexplicable, I don't really remember how it happened or why, but as we where walking home, I started to ask my dad why he treated me the way he did when I was younger? Why did he make me feel useless and worthless? These were and still are very important questions. I was very drunk and no answer would ever satisfy me. It was a disaster and I made a very bad error. I was horrible to my dad. I don't know where my aggression or anger came from. Perhaps it had been there all along. Of course I wanted to know why, but not like this. Not when I was incapable of understanding anyway! I told my dad that he had ruined the relationship with his dad and now he had destroyed his relationship with me. It was the alcohol speaking, but there was no excuse for that! We were approaching our house. I shook his hand and thanked him for ruining our relationship. I told him I would never speak to him again! He went home and I walked around for an hour, crying out loud in the rain.

The following day I woke up and knew straight away about the disaster the previous night. My intention was to get my things and ask my sister to drive away as soon as she could. She refused to drive away until I had spoke to my dad! I didn't want to face him. I felt, and rightly so, very ashamed. I ran into him in the garden by accident. I blurted out that I was very ashamed and very sorry. He told me that being drunk was the best way to get things off your chest. He told me he was a different person now to what he was then. I felt even worse because he was so understanding. I hugged him and apologised. I think I told him that I loved him. What a night! I only found out later that day that my two sisters' were fighting, literally fighting with each other also. They argued in the taxi home and continued when they were home! Never mix alcohol and families! Well, a little of both in moderation. I cried most of the way back to

Wales. I was distraught at my behaviour and the way I had treated my dad.

Once I actually got on with my job, as opposed to acting like a supervisor, I was actually very good at my new role. I had the added bonus of knowing I had gone away on several courses, and completed every one of them. I had passed them all, and more importantly I had a really good time and made some very good friends. That was important to me. Again, it proved I was normal and that I could have fun even when I was under pressure. So I was now completely and honestly recovered from my break-up. I was going out again and having fun. I had a couple of minor relationships in this period, but nothing serious. Nothing to brag about anyway.

Some time in 1999, I can't remember exactly when, my sister told me she was going to leave Warner and live in Portsmouth with her boyfriend at that time, Kev. I knew it was going to happen because she already told me about it. She worked for Warner for, and more particularly, at Bod since early 1993. There was a big leaving party for her. It took place in the paddocks, where I was now living. I loved living over there. The rooms were quite big and there were kitchens that the people in the house shared and there always seemed to be a party going on. As is the trend with 'surprise' parties, I think she already knew about it! It was another fantastic night. My second time at Bod was turning into something pretty special. Not quite as good as when I arrived in 1995, but I was really enjoying myself around that time. I made some really good friends, especially Ian and Stella, the bar manager and retail manager.

Things were okay. They weren't great. I was proud that I could take out, on a sunny day, up to forty, sometimes more people for an archery lesson. I made it fun and relaxing and I was really social. To stand up for twenty minutes and instruct can be daunting. But I enjoyed it. Yet, during all my feelings of happiness, spending time with my best friends etc, there was another side to me. I used to go back to my room, alone, and cry. Bitter frustrated tears. I couldn't understand why. I would put on a happy face in public, and then in private, the tears and sadness would flow out of me. I desperately wanted happiness. I deserved it. I felt like I was chasing my tail again.

I don't think it was deep down depression at this point because I had the strength to fight back and be at work the following day. I didn't feel like missing work. I loved my job. What I was going through wasn't depression, but it certainly was affecting me. On my own, in my room, I was really unhappy. Confusion is a cruel emotion. Apart from not having a girlfriend, I had everything I wanted. I cannot honestly say that I was having strong negative thoughts then. I was increasingly unhappy, but I didn't know why. I missed not having my sister around to talk to.

Before they left, my sister and her boyfriend had offered me the chance to move down to Portsmouth and live with them until I found my feet. I thought they were just being nice but the offer was still on the table a few months after my sister had gone. I think I wanted to try something new. In theory, I had everything to make me happy where I was. It wouldn't be too much longer until I would have been offered a management job somewhere in the company. At the time I felt disillusioned. I needed a break and I thought the best thing I could do was to cut my ties with Warner completely. I gave my notice in at around Christmas time 1999. I felt it was the right thing to do at that time. Still, I couldn't help thinking 'déjà vu'? The Christmas party was the best yet! It was my last so I made sure I enjoyed it!

I left Bodelwyddan Castle on 2nd February 2000. My dad came to pick me up. It wasn't as sad as I expected. I was ready to go. I was a better person when I left than when I arrived. Sadly, though, only just. Before the end, when

I left, I'd spent many an evening alone in my room, lost in thought. I was given another big leaving card and more importantly, I knew I would be welcome back. I called the place my home. I felt, most of the time, very relaxed there. As I wrote earlier, Bod is a magical place. I know now that it was a massive mistake to leave, but how was I to know that at the time? The plan was to go home for a few months and then move to Portsmouth and figure it out when I arrived. I wince when I read this aloud. I cannot quantify how much I gave up. And for what? I had no definite plans. I just wanted to get away from Wales. I was on the verge of becoming a manager. Less than a month after I left, my manager, Liz, decided to leave. Had I stayed, I probably would have been offered her job.

Sure enough, my stay down in Portsmouth was an absolute disaster! I moved in with my sister and her boyfriend and not long after that, they split up! I continued to live there, but I never felt comfortable. I got a job working behind a bar in the city. I was about as good at being a barman as I was at being a waiter! I needed a change, so I got a job working at C and A. I was a sales rep. I basically worked on the tills - which I wasn't too good at! I also worked on the shop floor. By this time, I was really, really struggling. I'm a very pragmatic person. I was then and I am now. I had given so much responsibility and potential in order to work in a shop! The money was poor and I couldn't put any fancy spin on the mistake I had made. I was back to not wanting to be seen in public. I felt awful. Much of this was, obviously, through unhappiness. More importantly though, where was my potential? While I was at Bod, I was studying a correspondence course in proof reading. My idea was to work in the day and study at night. This was definitely depression that I was suffering from. I couldn't find motivation or incentive anywhere. I was looking at what I had lost in terms of friends and prospects in Wales, instead of gritting my teeth, rolling up my sleeves and moving forward. I was making a habit of wallowing in self-pity. I had no fight left in me. Despite all the good from being in Wales, I mean the jobs and friends and girlfriend, when the questions were asked of myself, I had no answer. I buckled.

I eventually moved out of the flat my sister shared with her boyfriend and moved in with some lads that I worked with when I was at the pub. Had I been in a better frame of mind, I would have seen it as a positive step. I wasn't ever in a good frame of mind while I stayed in Portsmouth. A few days after I moved into my new address, I went out with some friends I made while I was at the pub. We all went to the Isle of Wight for the day. I wanted to go because I was in a full-scale war with depression at that point. I hadn't missed any days from work yet, but I was feeling more and more alone and isolated. I knew from previous experience that if I started to miss days off work and hid away, the next step would mean complete isolation, or worse. When I was out with these people, most of them younger than me, my mind was telling me I had no right to be with these people. Some of them were university students who worked part-time in the pub. My mind was telling me these were young and successful, while I was washed up. I had nothing to look forward to. I didn't deserve life because I had failed time and time again. All this was going on inside my head while I was sitting around the table. I had become well versed in faking smiles and laughing at the right time. This attack was stunning, even for me. It absolutely crippled me.

It wasn't long after that that my dad came all the way from Nottingham to pick me up and take me home. I don't think I ever really recovered from that day. I was heading back to Nottingham and back to the world I hated the most. I was going backwards, not forward. It was a world of hiding away because I was ashamed of who and what I was. Where was that person who had a good laugh and a girlfriend and friends not so long ago? I was the person I tried so hard not to become. I had been beaten by depression. It was the summer of 2000 that I returned home.

CHAPTER EIGHT
RELATIONSHIPS

When I arrived in Wales I was wide eyed and full of hope. I can't explain how or why, but I just knew that things would work out alright for me. Then, like now, women scare me. I don't mean I have any skeletons in the closet or a weird sexual history. I am a very naive when it comes to matters of the opposite sex. Well, I was when I arrived in Wales anyway. Because I had struggled with depression, I had believed that sex would prove me to be a real man and end all my problems with depression. No, it isn't quite as simple as that. For years I was told I was a good-looking lad. I received plenty of looks and offers from women. The problem was I put having sex on such a high pedestal, that it proved too high for me to reach! I did think that I become more relaxed once I got the deed out of the way. For a time, that did turn out to be the case. The idea of sex made me very nervous. I couldn't relax because I attached such a burden on it. I mean, I thought after having sex, most problems with depression would stop. The problem with this theory was that depression had become such a huge problem that the idea of being able to conquer it, or even some of it, became a big deal. Instead of viewing sex as natural or simply an act of enjoyment, I saw it as the solution to all my problems.

I was looking pretty sharp in my early days in Wales. I certainly had the talk, but I did have the walk. In fact, I had developed a pronounced stutter when I came to women! There was a waitress named Adele that I really liked. She liked me but I didn't have the guts to ask her out. Odd thing is, I could flirt with girls, but anything past flirting and the alarms would start ringing in my head. I knew Jinny, who was a dancer, liked me. She was really pretty, but I fancied Adele. One night after work, I was in the kitchen at the time, loads of us went out. I was grumpy because Adele wasn't there and she now had a boyfriend. I got drunk and ended up in Jinny's room. I fumbled and was too drunk to do anything anyway. I told her I was a virgin. It was said like it was a curse or something. I ended up spending the night in her room and when I woke the following morning, I sneaked away like a thief. God I was pathetic!

I was embarrassed that nothing had happened and I was concerned that she would tell everybody I was a virgin. I mean, so what! Looking back, it's no big deal. I was still only 22 years old. So I did the cowardly thing and tried to avoid her for the next few days. It was a pretty hard task because we lived in the same building and we were sure to see each other around the place! She wrote me a lovely, sweet letter and placed it under the pillow in my room. The contents of the letter was basically that I should get to know her before I decided that I didn't want anything to do with her - fair comment. She wanted me to meet her up the bar for a drink. I was petrified. I was going to have to face her at some point anyway. I decided to meet her at the bar. Actually, I had a really nice time. There was no pressure on me. She made me feel relaxed. I was really starting to like her. I told her that I didn't want a girlfriend and that we should be friends. I can't believe I used that line! In truth, I really fancied her and was angry, frustrated, disappointed. I took the easy way out. I was worried that if I commit myself to anything and I fall on my face, it would be a very long fall. I didn't want to let my sister down and I wanted to prove my parents wrong. It was a dangerous for me to become involved.

I really liked Jinny and as we saw much of each other, I got like her more. Flirting was safe because there was never any pressure on me to do anything. One Sunday, my best mate, Andy, left Bod. It was a huge blow to me because he was a real soul mate. I had told him a lot about my troubles because I needed somebody to confide in. I was gutted when he left. I really didn't want him to go. For a brief moment, I thought about begging him to stay! I hugged him goodbye and sadly watched until his little mini trundled out of view. That night I went out to the local pub with a lot of the staff. Jinny sat next to me and she knew that Andy's departure earlier that day was affecting my mood. I was on a table, in the middle section, and the table was vibrating with laughter. There was a good mood, apart from me. I dramatically rose and headed out the door. I was upset, but I knew Jinny was watching me all night. I was hurt and missing my best mate, but I also made the most of how that left me. I was drunk and I ran towards home. Jinny ran after me and called me back. Too late. I was quick and I decided to run to the beautiful graveyard in the village. It is where Jake, my elder sister's son is buried. It's a breathtaking site. There's a lovely marble church and the fact that, even though I was drunk, I still felt relaxed in the graveyard, will indicate that it's not your typical church. I went up to Jake's grave and Jake and me had a good old chatter. Of course, I did most of the talking. I told him I would not let anybody down. I would become made them proud. Yes I was drunk, but I wasn't totally paralytic. I bid Jake farewell and slowly made my way back to the staff corridor. The first person I saw was Jinny. She was worried about me and we went into my room and I told her I had been to see Jake. She turned to me and climbed on top of me. She kissed me and I returned her kiss. She looked at me and told me that we would 'take things slowly'. From that moment on, I had a 'proper girlfriend'.

Much to her credit, Jinny knew I was hung up about sex and she never made a big deal out of it. The first person I told was my sister. The Sunday I first kissed Jinny was the 5th February 1996. I had been in North Wales for nearly two months. Nothing had really worried me. I hadn't let anybody down.... yet. You see, I had such a bad few years before I arrived in Wales, I naturally expected something to go wrong. I just expected to let somebody down. I couldn't simply enjoy the good times while I had them. I was always concerned with how long it would be until I felt the familiar twinges of sorrow again.

It was not far off Valentines Day when I started seeing her. My sister took me out to buy her a card and a little present. It was funny because we hadn't had sex yet. We'd done certain things, but sex wasn't one of them. The card I needed had to be the right one. My sister told me that if I got her one with sexual overtones or smutty pictures, it might send the wrong signals. We spent a lot of time looking for one that contained sex and wasn't over the top on 'I love you's'. It was bloody hard! Jinny worked as a dancer in the entertainments department. She'd finish anywhere from midnight to two o'clock in the morning. At the time I was a lowly kitchen porter and I'd start work at about seven thirty in the morning, finish the morning shift at about midday. I would have to go back at around five thirty for the evening shift. I would finish that around nine o'clock at night. I had even more of a spring in my step now. My swagger and cockiness were bubbling and overflowing. I was really happy and very confident.... well, nearly very confident. I still hadn't done 'it' yet. We were sleeping together, either in my bed or her bed. It wasn't lack of effort on my part. I was always ready and willing.

It was in her room when 'it' finally happened. I won't go into detail, except to say that I cried afterwards. I had done it! I was a man now. The sky didn't open and no angles sang. No sign of a harp or fluffy white clouds! I cried because my Uncle, the one who I feared I was surely going to turn out like, had never had sex in his life. I'm not now and I wasn't then mocking, belittling or degrading him. I felt that I had proved to myself that I could perform in a relationship and I was adult enough to make a real stab at life. Jinny was moved. She knew I had a lot of issues but I'm not sure she knew how important it was for me to have finally have done 'it'. I wasn't disappointed. I did, however, wonder what all the fuss was about! With the holy grail now claimed, there was no stopping me now! I didn't feel that way. I expected to feel nothing immediately after I'd had sex, but I was expecting to become a calmer, more relaxed person because of it. I thought that the confidence that I'd gain from knowing I was like every other bloke would somehow redeem me. It's hard to convey what I expected after having sex for the first time. Certainly I didn't expect to have problems with depression again. In fact, I didn't for about fifteen months.

It was wonderful to be part of a couple. If I was invited anywhere, my girlfriend would also have an invitation. I loved simple things like going to the shops and buying things for her, things I knew she liked because I was her other half. It was what I wanted more than anything. To love somebody and to be loved in return. To make little jokes and buy silly little presents. That made me feel more comfortable with myself. We got the same day off together and we used to spend the mornings shopping in Rhyl and go out in the evenings. When I was at the bar, I would wait for her to finish and then we'd be together; as a couple. I was like everybody else. Instead of being bitter and jealous because I was on my own, I was relaxing and enjoying myself with somebody I learned to love very quickly. Contrast this with how I was feeling the same time the previous year. I was a completely different person. I had a pretty girl on my arm and I honestly couldn't have asked for more.

The girl she was sharing with, Kaggsie (her real name was Karen) moved into a different room. That left Jinny in a double room on her own. Unless she could share with somebody she liked, she may well have to share with somebody that she didn't like - it was a lottery. People didn't always share with people they liked. Anyway, Jinny asked me to move in with her! I was thrilled, although I didn't give her an answer straight away. Somebody, one of my mates, told me not to appear too keen. I kept her waiting a little longer than was needed before I told her I would love to move in. Another momentous moment in my recovery. To share my room with another girl was just so crazy! It was a big room with a double bed! That was a major bonus! It took me about thirty minutes to pack my things from my old room and walk up the corridor and put them in my new one. In the space of about 5 months, all my dreams had come true.

Everything was perfect. Then, one night I was in the gym, on the running machine. I still ran most days or nights. My appetite for fitness was even greater. I looked good. The man in mirror looked even better. Fitness, running especially, gave me a chance to reflect and take things easy. It was all going so well. I was in the gym and Jinny came to see me. She said she had something important to tell me. You could just tell it wasn't going to be good. Her face was really serious. In fact, she looked worried, perhaps even scared. She told me she'd be waiting in our room. It was a

Wednesday; our day off. I was feeling good until she told me she had something important to say to me.

I plodded over to our room. I knew that something was going to happen. She sat me down on the bed and she sat on the floor. I didn't look into her eyes. In my mind, I was thinking she already had a boyfriend and now she was leaving to join him. She told me she had lied to me. She paused and told she had phoned her mother and told her that she was going to tell me the truth. Oh my god. It was getting worse! Some family secret? I honestly felt sick. When I first met her, she told that she was a year younger than me, ie. 21. It may have 20. Her hideous secret was that she was, in fact, 17! Did I hear her correctly I asked myself. Did she just tell me she was seventeen? Was that it? Was that all she had to tell me? I laughed and hugged her. Big deal! She didn't look or act seventeen! I was delighted! I thought she might be pregnant or that she was going to tell me that she was leaving and going home! Her age didn't matter to me at all.

A few days later, I was much more shocked and scared to find out that Jinny's parents were coming to visit. "Wasn't that great news" she said? No, not really. I knew she was close to both her parents. Her mother phoned her three times a week. I walked past the phone once when they were talking and the conversation was about 'socks.' fact whenever the phone in the corridor was ringing, most people left it for Jinny to answer because it was probably for her anyway! I was worried. I had never met nor spoken to her parents before but that didn't take away the fear. Fear of what? I think it's the fear of not measuring up. Not being able to satisfy her mum and dad that I was a good lad and good enough for their daughter. I told her that I would go out and meet them that very night. I asked her to finish as early as possible. I didn't want to have to sit and make superficial conversation for too long. There was no way I could meet them sober. I needed dutch courage and lots of it. Of course, too much courage and they'd definitely not like me. I needed to be merry.

I finished that night around nine, showered and changed and up the bar for about nine-thirty. My plan was to drink about three pints in about half an hour! I think I was on my third pint when Jinny introduced me to them. We sat and made polite small talk. Jinny was on a break, but kept looking at her watch. She didn't have long. Watching her looking at her watch made me anxious. She left us and went back to work. She kissed me and told me she'd only be a couple of hours and then she'd join us. It was down to me to make the right impression. I was on my own.

The cavalry arrived in the form of my sister. She was drunk and interrupted a conversation about something really boring. She was a breathe of fresh air. She introduced herself as my sister and made us all feel much more relaxed. Well, she made me feel much better anyway. She kept apologising for being drunk and told us she'd leave us to talk. Jinny's father, Chris, didn't want her to go. Both of them enjoyed my sister's company and I think they knew it made me feel more relaxed having her there. When she did leave, I felt much stronger and I was able to relax and be myself. They liked me, of course they did. I was even more relieved when Jinny sat with us. She finished her shift and stayed with us for the rest of the night. She sat next to me and held my hand as we all talked and laughed. I stroked her golden hair, as I always did, and her father looked at me and explained that his daughter wasn't a dog. I laughed. I was in a much better frame of mind. My sister had helped me once again and given me much needed courage and strength. I thought then, as I thought many a time after, how would I ever have survived without my big sister.

It was something that I got used to. Her parents came to see her a lot. The more I met them, the more relaxed I became. What worried me most was her parents' attitude to someone six years their daughters senior and a person with a shady past and perhaps, an even less certain future. They both new I was a keen writer. By this time, I was studying a correspondence writing course. The concern was my job at present. I was a kitchen porter. I served teas and coffees and cleaned plates. Was I good enough for their daughter? They never mentioned it. They read some of my short stories and offered me positive comments. I was relieved, but still not happy with what I was doing. I believed I could achieve more, so much more, as long as I had Jinny with me.

My parents came up to see my sister and me. You can be sure that was a bundle of high energy and excitement. This was one step beyond the time at Christmas that I went home all proud and dandy. Their visit went well. They liked Jinny and she liked them. Before they left, I promised that we would visit them soon. How my heart beat with pride. I mean it beat savagely, out of control. I was telling them that I was going to go home and that I would bring my girlfriend along. Yes, I see how simple that statement was to formulate and say. It was a measure of my continuing improvement as a person. I had never believed that I would ever take a girl home with me. Now I was in a position to promise my parents that I would do just that!

As I stated before, my girlfriend and her parents were very close. I think it was because she was young and she was living away from home. It had been arranged that her dad would drive to Wales, from Leicester, and pick us up. After breakfast and a cup of tea, he would drive us all the way back to Leicester, where Jinny and I would stay for a few days. We had both booked the time off and were really looking forward to getting away for a while. I was sort of looking forward to it. By this time I had met her parents on many occasions. Still, going to their house, their territory, and being calm and relaxed was something that worried me. My attitude was always doom and gloom first. I always, and still do, look at a glass half empty. I look at possible consequences before I look for the benefits. If things go wrong, how will they affect me? What will it do to my self-confidence? All the way there in the back of her dad's car, she held my hand. She knew I was worried about the occasion. She just smiled and laughed at me. Not harshly though. She told me I was being silly. She was right. I was welcomed into their home and I felt guilty pretty much straight away.

I relaxed and enjoyed myself. I was also taught what is and is not permitted by boyfriend and daughter under her parents' roof. We slept on a single bed again and however much I pleaded and sulked, there was no 'hanky panky' of any description. That really annoyed me. Put me in a mood. Still there was no point in sulking about it. She took me out to see some of her old friends from school and a dance college that she used to attend. I enjoyed the attention. It took my mind off other things that had annoyed over the last few days. I felt really proud of myself. I was shown off and paraded like a prize horse. I loved it! I craved the attention. For years I didn't have any attention so now I was becoming addicted to it! I met her brother, who, for some reason, didn't seem to like me. We were about the same age, 23. Remember I had promised my mother that I would go and see her too. This was on the Saturday, the day after we were picked up by her dad. Her mother, Lorraine, was a cook in a school kitchen. Whenever her parents came to visit us in Wales, her mother used to bring loads of cakes! I told her I had to watch my weight and be careful because I was a diabetic. I'd say that, but I had no problem with eating them! That Saturday, her mother was busy in the kitchen preparing our dinner for that evening. It really smelled great. Of course, by train, the distance between Nottingham and Leicester is only about thirty minutes away. That was great because it meant we could spend a few hours with my parents and then hop on the train and be back in Leicester in no time.

As we left the train and travelled in the back of the taxi, heading towards my home, I felt a surge of pride. I had my arm around my girlfriend and I was telling her about my house and that my dad always had a car outside the house and one, battered old wreck up the drive. It was always the same. Fairly nice car outside and a battered wreck up the drive. It made me laugh and filled me with pride in equal measures. My mum and dad hugged us both and we sat around chatting excitedly. I told them about work and this and that and my dad was fascinated with Jinny because she could do the splits! He used to study Karate, years ago. He used to sit on the floor, legs crossed in front of him, and ask me to stand on each knee! He was trying to get his knees parallel with the floor. His aim was, eventually to be able to do the splits! He never did succeed though! When I saw what my mother had prepared I wanted to cry in frustration. She told me proudly that she had been busy all morning making cakes and preparing a buffet for all of us. It was in honour of Jinny and me coming to visit. I felt so useless. There was a beautiful array of food set out on plates and trays on the kitchen top. She must have spent a long time getting it all ready. We couldn't eat too much because Jinny's mother had cooked a big meal back in Leicester. I told my mother that we had a meal waiting back in Leicester. She gave me a beautiful, radiant smile and told me that it wouldn't go to waste. I felt guilty because of all the trouble she had gone to. On the taxi, heading back to the station, I said very little. Jinny and I had a little argument over it. Still, there was nothing I could do. In another hour or so, we were going to eat a roast meal. My appetite was strangely absent.

When we arrived back in Wales, I could reflect that things went really well. Nothing had happened that would lead to severe embarrassment! It was approaching Christmas time 1996. For the first time in decades I was actually looking forward to it. It would be my first with my girlfriend and it really felt, at the time, that it was my first proper Christmas since I was a kid. We hd moved rooms again, to the room in the middle of the corridor. It was where all the noise and music emanated from, the centre of activity, where everyone gathered. Everybody seemed excited about Christmas that year. It was the last big celebration that we would have together. At least half of the people on the corridor were leaving for some reason or other. It was the last chance to enjoy each other's company. I spent quite a lot of money on presents that year. Most of it was spent on my girlfriend. A really odd thing happened to me. I usually don't like spending money on other people. I was so used to living on my own. Yet on our days off approaching Christmas, we would each go on our own and buy gifts for each other. It was fun when we met up about an hour later and we each looked at the size of the package and number of bags we were carrying. It was impossible to tell what might be my present, and what might be groceries, but it was certainly a lot of fun.

On Christmas day itself I spent the early hours with my arm draped across Jinny thinking of the previous night. We went with nearly the entire staff corridor meeting us at the bar. I didn't get drunk. I was already too happy to need alcohol. It was an early night. We all said goodbye before midnight and went to bed. It was the first time I'd ever done anything like that. Go out on Christmas Eve and feel happy and looking forward to what was to come. How different this was from last year! And sure enough, the happiness was about to come to an end.

There were loads of presents placed around the little tree in our room. You could easily tell them apart. Jinny's presents for me were immaculately wrapped. Tight, with no obvious seams. There were little bows and cute ribbons. There were little labels with my name on them. They were an art form in themselves. They looked so nice, I felt guilty about having to open them. Yet, my greedy side took over and I thought 'sod it, they're my presents under all that'. All my presents to Jinny appeared to be big and bulky objects. They weren't, it was just that I used so much wrapping paper and there were bits of cello tape sticking out everywhere. My sister had offered to wrap them for me. I wished I took her up on the offer.

Jinny opened my presents to her first. Another new experience for me. To watch somebody's face, a person you love, and see a mixture of excitement, apprehension and then outright joy and happiness was an incredible experience for me. I was getting all excited about her getting all excited. She did comment on my wrapping, but as I pointed out, the paper only goes into the bin anyway. I cannot remember what I bought for her. It was lots of little presents and one or two more expensive ones. She hugged me and thanked me. Now was time for the real fun: it was my turn to open the presents that she'd gotten for me! I was really excited about this. It was one big present and a few little ones. Wanting to prolong the anticipation, I opted to open the little ones first. I was like a man possessed. Hurling the tightly wrapped paper in the air to get at my prize. At last it was the big one. It was a large box and its contents were not too heavy. I'd been picking it up and analysing its mass and structure every time I was alone in our room. She watched my expectantly.

I had a good idea what it was. She knew I really wanted a Play Station. I hinted to her while we were shopping in Liverpool. When I opened the box, I looked at her in shock.

It wasn't a Play Station. It was a midi hi-fi centre. I had told her, months before, that I would buy my own hi-fi. I planned on getting a really good one. I couldn't hide my disappointment. I was like a young kid about to cry. I just didn't think. The first thing I said to her was something like 'what did you get me one of these for? I told you I'd buy my own'. She looked really upset. She opened the door and walked out. She didn't yell or slam the door. I felt really bad. I had been selfish and stupid. She was on the phone to her mom within minutes. When I apologised and we had made up, I saw my sister in the shop and told her what happened. Boy, did she go for my throat! She told me what I had already told myself, that I was selfish and stupid!

Even though she was six years my junior, Jinny was really mature. I couldn't help but open up to her. She didn't judge me. She just listened to what I had to say. It was great for me that I could talk to somebody about things that had tormented me for years and not feel ashamed or embarrassed at the same time. It was like talking to a 'shrink.' She allowed me to get loads of grief off my chest. We had decided to accept the offer of work at the new hotel. I wasn't sure, but I kept my reservations to myself. If she was going to go so was I. I know it was a mistake that I went because I hated being at Littlecote. Even with hindsight, I wouldn't have changed my mind. I really did love her and I didn't want to be without her. She was my fist love and I suppose I wanted to make the most of this situation while I could. I was a much happier, more confident person when I was with her. Sure we argued, but then so did everybody.

Before we left for Littlecote, Jinny and I went to stay with my mum and dad for a few days. It was lovely and relaxing. Oddly, we didn't go out. I mean at night, drinking or at the movies. It was something I really wanted to do. Be seen in my hometown with a lovely young girl on my arm. We were forced to share a single bed again, this time because my little sister refused to let me and Jinny have her bed for a couple of nights! In the end, I did the manly thing and slept on the floor.

I didn't join Jinny until a week after she had arrived at Littlecote. One of our friends picked me up from the station and before we drove to the hotel, we stopped off and got something to drink for later. I was really pleased to see Jinny. It had only been a week but I had missed her. The following day, with my girlfriend on my arm, I was given the tour of the new hotel. Even then, I had to feign excitement. Everybody seemed genuinely thrilled to be a part of this new hotel. I tried to be as thrilled as others, including my girlfriend, but it was hard. Still, I was going to give it a real go. I wanted things to work out. The first week I was there all of the staff were generally tidy the place up and helping out were they could. The hotel was not officially ready for business but it would open a few days after I arrived. There was a big party to welcome all the new staff and the atmosphere was friendly and lively. However, our room was really small and we eventually swapped with a couple of girls. This new room was out of the way of the main staff accommodation.

Right from the start, I really struggled to make friends. I still had the friends who came down from Wales. The new hotel attracted new staff from existing hotels. Warner, at that time, had a dozen hotels in the British Isles. So at first, it was quite clannish. The staff that came down from a certain hotel tended to stick with that hotel's staff. I was feeling a little lost. I wasn't unhappy, but you can't kid yourself for long. I joined a good gym in the nearest town, Hungerford. I bought myself a bike, because it was about three miles to Hungerford and I couldn't be bothered to walk all the time. I hated the place from a very early on. Even typing these words now, I still hate the place! There was a big difference in attitude at this hotel. I was happy in Wales. I was relaxed and at ease. Jinny, however, was much happier at this new hotel. From an early stage I could see she was growing more and more confident and she was the one who was making new friends. Our new room was away from the main staff block, but more and more often, Jinny was going over to the staff block for a party or just to hang around other people's rooms. I didn't really do that. I stayed in our room and in the end I was happy just to have a few mates and a girl I loved.

We went on holiday to Crete and that was a really proud moment for me. It was my first time on a plane and it was my first time abroad. I was a bit grumpy because I had lost the toss and couldn't have the window seat! On the other hand it was a nighttime flight so not much could be seen anyway. We needed a good holiday because things weren't going so well between us. We argued a lot, but then again, we were arguing most of the time anyway by now. I wanted it to work on holiday. Perhaps I got used to having a girlfriend and didn't think I needed to impress her anymore. It was worse because for some reason I couldn't talk to my girlfriend any more. Looking back, I feel sorry for her. I was a miserable bastard at the hotel and I found it hard to smile on holiday.

We didn't even have the same day off anymore. I had Sundays off and she had Saturdays - that didn't help. The Christmas of 1997 was horrible. How things change! 1995 was horrendous, 1996 was brilliant, and 1997 was horrible. I bought her a ring. It was really expensive. We needed a good Christmas because the holiday wasn't great and I think we both knew that we were growing apart. It wasn't a good Christmas because I had to share her with her parents and one of her best friends. We were all squeezed into our room. I was bitterly disappointed. Not so much with her parents being there (although, her parents were always there), but I wanted her on her own. Her friend Allison was in the way. She was in my way, anyway. In return for an expensive ring, I got, well, not very much. She could see I was disappointed, though I tried to smile through it. She explained that she had so many presents to buy. I thought to myself it didn't stop her buying a decent present the previous year! It all added up to a crap day! She had changed, and grown up a bit. The New Year was nothing special. By this time, I was really struggling. I knew I wasn't happy and I couldn't see much hope in my future at Littlecote.

Jinny was very honest. I'll give her that. She was also getting sick of working down there. However, her reason was to do with her job and not the place itself. One night I was out with her and her mum and dad made another surprise visit! I really liked her parents but they were always around. I was like they didn't want their daughter out of their site for too long. We were sitting around a table and Jinny and I were generally badmouthing Warner, the company that employed us. Suddenly, Jinny said something along the lines of that it didn't matter how her manager treated her because she was leaving to work on cruise ships soon. That was the first that I'd heard of that idea. I looked across at her, and she looked white. She met my eyes and apologised. I was very sober and I felt numb. I really did feel sick. I got up without saying a word and walked away. Jinny ran after me to explain but I wasn't interested. I was really hurting. Everything was falling apart for me here.

This is where I really needed faith in myself. I had achieved so much in such a short space of time. I was a better person and I did have a future. Unfortunately, I was swamped in sadness. I felt very low and I knew, I just knew that things were about to get worse. In the early months of 1998, around mid-February, a lot of staff went out together, me and Jinny included. I got drunk because I was feeling really unhappy. It was a big night because the star cabaret was the late, great Bob Monkhouse. He was brilliant.

After the show, Jinny came up to me to tell me that many of the staff were complimenting me on my body. I know this sounds vain. I was at the gym on a regular basis and I was wearing a top that was a few sizes too small. I was nasty to her and told her to leave me alone. I walked home drunk and very alone. That was the last straw. I must admit, I was becoming more and more negative and closing in on myself. I had changed a lot. I wasn't as positive and the laughs that Jinny and I used to have seemed to have completely dried up. I was not the same enthusiastic, energetic person I was in Wales. I felt desperately upset because I was fully aware of what was happening, and what was going to happen. I simply watched it unfold in front of my eyes.

The following day was Sunday, my day off. I rode to Newbury and brought Jinny a video that I knew she wanted. When I got back I surprised her with it and some silly little things too. You know, cuddly toys and strange things that girls seem to like. It was my way of apologising for the previous night. I was called into work because somebody was sick. Jinny didn't want me to go in. I didn't want to go in, but I had to. When I returned, Jinny was at work. There was a letter on the bed. I walked up slowly and read it. She'd had enough. Things weren't the same and it wasn't fun anymore. I was absolutely devastated. I cried out loud and I cried into my hands. I couldn't stop comparing this letter with the one that she'd written for me in Wales. Granted, the contexts were very different, but still, I kept comparing them. I begged her to change her mind. No way. We were friends after, but I hated the place even more. This is the first time that I really, really hated myself. It may have been that we'd drift apart anyway, but I was so downbeat and negative. I know the break-up was my fault. I thought that because I had a girlfriend that I didn't need to carry on treating her special. I was more concerned about how I was feeling than what was happening to my relationship with my girlfriend. I don't blame her for 'dumping' me. I wasn't a happy person to be around.

I tried to 'patch' things up but it was too late. I still loved her and I wanted her back. She continued to say no and the final straw was when I saw her smile at this lad in the kitchen. It's hardly a hanging offence, but those smiles used to be mine and I couldn't stand the thought of her giving anybody else the same attention. I was going to quit the hotel. We still went out together as friends. That was really breaking my heart. She was really happy and I wasn't. She told me she was leaving soon anyway. In the end, I left before she did. I cried very hard when we said goodbye. She hugged me and told me that she loved me. Oh how that hurt to hear. I went back to Wales and got my old job back straight away. I have never had a proper girlfriend since. I have never had sex with another girl since. I never really recovered from that experience. I have never felt as proud of myself as I did when we were a couple. I think the real eye opener was the way I fell apart even when I had a girlfriend! At one point in my life, I had all I wanted and I still wasn't happy.

CHAPTER NINE
HOME AGAIN

I left Wales in 2000 on a cold February morning. I went back home for a brief spell before I went to Portsmouth. As I said before, leaving Wales when I did was a costly mistake. Within three months of arriving in Pompey, I was back home again and I didn't have a clue what I as going to do with my life. I did what I do best these days. I simply hid in my room and lived off benefits. I didn't see any doctors or shrinks. Whenever I spoke to my doctor, the best he could offer me was anti-depressant pills and a very long wait until I got to speak to a therapist. The pills were giving me some incredible dreams. Many of them were about flying. I slept a lot in that period because sleeping can't hurt; reality can. At some point I recovered enough to go back to work and, at least, rediscover some pride. It was the usual kind of work for me. Labouring or working in a warehouse. I did the usual act. I laughed on cue and smiled when I thought it was right. I felt like a zombie. I had no commitment to any kind of life. I do not know how I survived. This time, the thought of college wasn't exactly the shimmering holy grail that it was when I was younger. I was older and much more cynical now. I'm not happy to admit that. I don't trust many people or concepts. I had turned into a bitter young man who was constantly raging with the world. I was living at home again, and although I was part of the household, I felt more like part of the furniture. My parents rarely saw me. My little sister had left to work on a holiday centre. Another one bitten by the holiday centre curse! I'm not sure if I told my parents about my plan to return to college. Sadly, I told them very little about what was happening in my life. It's hard to make conversation with anybody, including your parents, when inside, you feel beaten and at a loss.

I enrolled in an 'Access to Higher Education' course at Nottingham's Clarendon College. The course was designed for mature students, that is those people who were over twenty-one, to study for nine months on a course specially designed to give them the qualifications to go onto university. My heart lurched forward and as soon as I learned of this course, I had visions of conquering the world and national holidays being named after me. The thought of having to do less than a year really spurred me on. I was working at that time and it made life much more easy to handle. I mean, just for a while, I was having happy thoughts of me actually going on to university. I went to an interview and it got off to a great start when I told the woman who was interviewing me my age - I was 27 at the time. She looked at me and said I looked much younger. Who doesn't like to hear that they look 'much younger' than they actually are? That was music to my ears. I cracked a few jokes, settled into my seat, as oppose to sitting stiffly upright. Just a compliment made me feel totally different.

She read the work I had prepared for her, a short written account of my emotions as I watched Liverpool Football Club beat Wycombe Wanderers in the first round of the F.A Cup. She smiled and told me she was really impressed and welcomed me onto the course. The course was set to start in the middle of September 2001. It was roughly two months before the start of the course that I attended the interview. I'd done it. I didn't doubt that I would. I had about two months to slim down and get ready for this course. I couldn't possibly start college looking the way I did at that point! I was overweight and I was a mess. This was the catalyst I needed to get me back on the road again. I felt much better, but sadly, absolutely miles away from the person I was at the start of my time in Wales.

The Access course had four main elements to it: Biology, Psychology and sociology. There was also a section on Information Technology and dreaded MATHS! Maths and me do not go together. On the first day there was nearly thirty people in the class. The ages ranged from twenty-one to fifty. I was relieved that I wasn't the oldest person in the class. As usual on first days, everybody had to stand up in front of everybody else and say a little about themselves and why they wanted to go on to university. I reacted like everybody else. When it was my turn I stood up and delivered, in a calm, confident voice who I was and what I'd done in my past. I gave my reasons and I had done well. After all, I was the same person who used to instruct archery, rifle shooting and fencing.

I enjoyed some of the subjects that I was taking. Biology, to my surprise, was really good. The teacher and the subject were really interesting. It was something I had to pay close attention to because I'm not a technical or scientific person. Sociology was okay. I was able to write some really good assignments. I think I was strong in that subject because it involved work that dealt with opinions and being subjective. There was also an English lesson a couple of times a week. English is where I excelled at college. My work was of a very high standard and I knew I could deliver the 'goods'. That was a great feeling for me. I had been through another really bad patch. I was proud of myself because under all the stress and pressure I was under, I still produced, especially in English and Sociology, some very good work.

I was feeling a lot better about myself. During the course, we all had to decide what course we wanted to study and what university. The idea is that each person applied to six universities. That way, if the one you really wanted to attend turned you down, you'd at least have five other possibilities. There was loads of paperwork to fill in, and unfortunately for me, this meant neat and legible handwriting. We were advised to fill in the forms in pencil first, and then go over the pencil in black biro. I didn't like it one bit. It took time and patience and of course the ability to be able to write. That ruled me out on all three counts! I'm not patient and I'm definitely not neat. It took me a few days of swearing and threatening our cat before I finally finished! When it came to writing an account of why I should be accepted at the universities that I had chosen, I was brilliant. All six universities that I applied for offered my a place on the course. That was the good news. The bad news was that they were all conditional offers, which means they would only accept me if I passed maths as well as gaining my Access to Higher Education certificate. I knew I was going to get my access certificate, but, well, maths and I were going through a rough time. We had so many break ups that I wasn't sure we would ever get back together again! I needed a miracle.

The course that I decided I wanted to do at university was criminal Psychology. I have always been fascinated by why people commit murders and savage acts of violence. Problem was, even though I knew I was going to pass the Psychology part of the course, I didn't really enjoy that subject as much as I thought I would. Considering I was about to commit myself to a three year course, at one of six universities, I was going to have to find the subject much more interesting.

I'd made some really good friends on the course. I felt good and pretty relaxed most of the time. Physically, I was sto;; struggling with my weight. I was maybe a stone overweight. Despite the fact that my performances in class and my overall work was of a really high standard, the way I looked was getting me down. I was still running at night and keeping myself fairly fit, but I felt uncomfortable in public. It sickens me now, when I reflect, because it makes no difference. My work was brilliant and for that I was proud of myself. However, I was still unhappy. I went out a few times with some of the guys from the group. On one occasion we were all celebrating the end of our first term. We had to hand in a huge Sociology assignment and the lads all went out into Nottingham city centre on the same evening. Before I went out, I was in my room, drinking cider, trying to relax before I met the others. I was trying on my clothes and seeing what I looked best in. It was a squeeze to fit into my favourite trousers. I had put weight on and I knew it would be a squeeze. I stared at myself in the mirror and was disgusted by what I saw. I hated myself for looking fat and not being able to put on the trousers.

All the good work and effort I had put in to my course work went out the window. I saw this image in front of me that I hated. I sank to my bed, as I was totally deflated. Still, I was determined to go out and try and enjoy myself. I walked two miles into town and I felt really uncomfortable. The fact that once again, the person in the mirror was somebody I wished wasn't there, affected my thinking. Instead of relaxing and enjoying myself, I ended up hating and calling myself names in the mirror. I can't help it when this happens. I met the other guys and tried to enjoy myself. No chance. They were all happy and excited and I was grinning like the village idiot because if I didn't, I would have sat there with one of my miserable faces. When we were walking to another pub, I sneaked away when their backs were turned and I caught the bus home. Usually I'd walk home, but I felt so deflated that I couldn't be bothered. It was a Friday night so at least I didn't have to go into college the next day. It hurts when that happens. It's heartbreaking because I pick myself up and I continually allow myself to be dragged down again.

I fought my way back in terrific style. In English, one of the assignments was to write a short story. I rubbed my hands in anticipation. I could do well in this, and I knew it. If the individual wanted, their story could be read out by the teacher to the rest of the class. That's what I needed. An audience to listen to my work. If it went well, I would be left feeling pretty good. After the disastrous night out, I needed cheering up. Positive reinforcement, we'd done it in Psychology. That's what I needed. The teacher marked my work and she told me it was 'excellent'. She then asked me if she wanted me to read it to everybody else? I was nodding my head, frantically, as soon as she started the sentence. I sat at the front of the class with the teacher. She began reading and I stared into my twitching hands. This was a huge moment for me. I had decided that I wanted the teacher to read my work out because she said it was excellent and I believed that it would be well received by all my peers. If I was wrong, and it wasn't the success I desperately needed it to be, it would turn into a disaster. I would be so hurt and wounded, I would leave the classroom and I would not turn in for a few days. I wanted people to tell me that they really liked my work. The story was called 'Operation Dirty Betty'. It's about a desperate young man who is forced to go into a chemist and buy some condoms for his night of passion with the exotic 'Dirty Betty'. It was a comedy so I was desperately pleading to hear laughter.

I was asking a hell of a lot: for my work to be well received and laughed at. It was, without doubt, my proudest moment ever! Everybody laughed. And the laugher was loud and long. I soared with pride. I felt so strong and glad to be alive. The room was quiet before my story was read out. I had gambled and I'd come out on top. At that point, I can see how desperate I am to hear positive compliments about myself. I think it's because I feel so low about myself, to hear other people contradict my own thoughts is a real shot in the arm for me.

Towards the end of the course, I was drowning in self-pity again. I was struggling to attend and I was very unhappy. I was sitting a mock maths exam. I needed a good result to lift my spirits. I know now that it's ridiculous to put myself under so much pressure. I couldn't live with that pressure. I was very unhappy before I started the exam and on the second page was really tough, a right bastard of a question on algebra (aren't they all!). I never used algebra in my life and to crack up because of an algebra question was too much! I threw all my things into my bag and stormed out. I was so angry that I didn't even apologise to my maths teacher! I rode home to an empty house and cried. I had affectively walked out on college. Yes, theoretically I could return on the Monday. I knew I wouldn't. I felt empty and I knew that I had no more to give. I had hit bottom again and as far as I was concerned, my attempt to go to university was a pathetic waste of time - just like my life.

It was nearly two weeks until I heard from my college tutor. I told her over the phone that I was suffering from depression and I couldn't finish the course. I told her I couldn't do anymore and I didn't want to study Psychology anyway! I said it in a petulant, whiney voice! She asked me to come see her and I told her that I would. Margaret, my tutor, convinced me to finish the course and get my certificate. I whined that I couldn't see myself finishing maths. She told me not worry about that. If I didn't want to study Psychology, I didn't have to take maths; that produced a grin on my face. Margaret convinced me that my talents were with English. Why didn't I consider taking an English course at university instead? I agreed. However, it was too late to go to University that year for me. Not technically. I could still apply for an English course and apply in September 2002. Yet, I didn't want to go that year. I felt like crap and had no confidence. I thought it best that I try and get my head straight and then go to university in 2003. So I finished the course and said good luck to all of the friends I'd made. They were all going to university that September and I felt pretty dejected. I really wanted to go to university, but I knew that I was struggling at that moment and I wouldn't have been a good idea for me to go just then.

I passed the course. I was down, but at least I knew that I could to university the following year. It felt good to know that I had the qualification to enter university. The hard work had been done. The problem I had to contend with now was what was I going to do until September of 2003 when the new term started. That was easy. Nottingham is infested with employment agencies. I would simply get a job with one of those. However a problem was developing. My employment record since I'd left Wales was not good. I worked for a lot of firms, mainly employment agencies. I was forced to quit work on so many occasions because of my problems with depression, yet I didn't want to tell my prospective employers that I was unreliable because of depression. It worried me then and it does now. My employment record is awful because I always end up leaving work and claiming sickness benefit.

The Christmas and New Years of 2003 was okay. I didn't try and kill myself, which is a good start for the New Year. My plan for 2003 was to find work and earn some money before I left for university. Of course, this new plan needed some direction. Where was I going to go? Which university and which course? At the start of the year, I had no idea of the answers to these questions. I was feeling okay at this point. I remember I was working at B & Q and I was talking to this lad, Robert, who used to go to the same school as I did. I told him, with burning pride and real honesty, that I was only working there for a short time, up until July or so, and after that, I was going to university. By that time, which made me feel even better, I decided what course and at what university I was going to attend. I had decided on Southampton Institute being the university and the course was Media Writing. This was an English media based course. While I was working at B & Q I had recovered some of my swagger. Only very slightly though. I was still overweight and I was still unhappy, but I was working and now I had a plan and direction.

Sadly, my time at B & Q was cut short. I was unfortunate to have a diabetic 'fit' while I was at work. They let me go. I cycled home and I was pretty down about my end at B & Q. To cheer myself up, I stopped off in the city and bought loads of chocolate. That night, I was genuinely upset. I ate all the chocolate to 'drown my sorrows'. Had I had any friends or more confidence, I would have gone out drinking with them. I ended up in hospital because I messed up the amount of insulin to combat all the chocolate I ate. More evidence of my up and down life. The paramedics asked me if I tried to kill myself. The answer was no. I had a lot to live for so that was out of the question. My chief regret was yet again I had worried my parents. I don't think they believed that I tried to kill myself but since I arrived at home, after my time in Wales, I had a lot of problems with my diabetes. I spent quite a few hours in hospitals. My dad was always there for me. On this occasion both my parents came to the hospital with me. That is saying a lot because it was about three o'clock in the morning. I had pulled the same stunt many times before. Never intentional; I mean I didn't overdose on insulin, although I have tried it before.

My dad was always the one who waited at the hospital for me. He has always been the one who came to pick me up when I fell apart and wanted to come home. I owed him so much. I know after all I've divulged that these words seem hypocritical, but by now, my dad had changed massively.

It wasn't long until I was fighting back and got myself another job. It was a job that entailed wrapping tables and chairs in protective bubble wrapping. Again, I told them 'I wouldn't be here too long because I'm off to university in September.' It was a strange time because even though my reflection in the mirror told me that I looked like crap; in my heart, I was excited about going to university.

I went back to Wales a few times in the times after I had departed from Bod. My elder sister and I went back in August of 2003. My best friends in Bod, Stella and Ian were having an engagement party and my elder sister and I were invited. I said that it would be good if our dad came as well. I cannot remember why I didn't suggest my mother as well. I guess I didn't think that it was her kind of scene. So, my dad, my elder sister and I all travelled to North Wales in my dad's car. My sister was driving and my dad was in the passenger seat. He was moaning, but with a smile on his face, about my sister's driving speed.

We left early on Saturday morning. It wasn't the first time I'd gone back. I'd been back on three or four other occasions. One of which was especially memorable because it involved me being attacked by a crazy woman in a nightclub! That was weird. Even more bizarre was the fact that the crazy woman happened to be my sister! Too much alcohol, that's all I'm going to say. I always enjoyed myself when I returned to Wales. My dad had joked with my sister about being shocked that it was my idea that he should come to Wales with us. He told me he was really surprised that I should come up with the idea. I think he was really thrilled to be coming with us. It as an incredible weekend. I was on a high. A proper, genuine, no strings attached good mood. I was relaxed and in high spirits all weekend. I didn't want to leave at the end of it. At every opportunity I was telling anyone who would listen about my going to university in the coming September. I told everybody that was at the party and any poor, unsuspecting person I bumped into over the weekend. It was especially important for me to broadcast this news to people that I used to work with. I wanted them to know that I was on my way to a better life. I looked good and I felt alive. It's hard to describe fully what I mean about being so 'alive'. For the past few years I had dragged myself through life. Years of facing a figure in the mirror who I pretended wasn't me. Countless mornings where I wished I didn't just surface from a dream, only to be back in reality and back to being me. Being alive at that moment meant that I could face people. I could stand up and be counted because I had some purpose in life. I felt 'alive' because I was truly living. I was experiencing laughter and music and smiles. It was a great time for me.

My dad got dressed up and he really looked very sharp. I was proud of him. He danced and clapped his hands and sang the wrong words to songs. I got drunk and enjoyed the moment. It was really important for me. My dad, for the first time in a very long time, saw a different side of me. He was used to the person who hid in the shadows and never went out. The person who laughed rarely and smiled even less. The person he saw in Wales was the person I aspired to be. Unfortunately, I haven't been 'that' person again since that time.

In July 2003, I had a chance to visit the university on one of their open days. To be honest, I wasn't thrilled at the thought of travelling all way down to Southampton and then having to come all the way back again the same day. The tour started at midday on a Wednesday. My sister, again, came to my rescue. She told me that she had a really good mate who lived in Portsmouth who said he was willing to use his day off to take me over to the university in Southampton. Even better was the news that I could stay at his place for the night. Of course I was delighted with this news. I meant that I could travel down and not have to rush back. I was looking forward to seeing the place. I read and heard so much about it, now I could add substance and texture to all my dreams. Because I was doing the map reading, my sister's mate and I got lost, somewhere in Southampton city centre. Lucky for us the university, well actually it was the Southampton Institute, was only five minutes from the city centre.

I was seriously excited while the tour was in progress. I had to clench my fists to calm down. Here I was. I'd made it. This is what I had been waiting for and I was duly impressed. The tour consisted of lecture halls and other facilities including the library and gym. I listened with enthusiasm to some of the lecturers. I even asked a question and I was told that it was a good question. I was on a roll! I left really impressed with what I'd seen. That night I went for a run, because I needed to let some of my excitement go. I brought the lad some beers and thanked him for the use of his spare room and for coming with me. I slept very well that night.

My best friend, throughout my life, was my big sister. I didn't go out much at home, unless it was with my dad and elder sister. I didn't have a 'proper' friend anywhere in site at this time. I felt like a character in a kids cartoon, a cheesy American cartoon where the main character is a fat, lonely kid with glasses and all he wants is a friend! Sadly though, the friends in the cartoon world usually turned out to be talking cats or dogs or monsters. Even that would have been an improvement for me. I was friendly and social at work. I was pretending most of the time to relax. I never really felt comfortable anywhere I worked. I wouldn't go out with the 'lads' for a drink because I didn't like the way I looked. I felt fat and bloated and I simply didn't want go out and continue acting. The only concession I was prepared to make was to stay in and drink. That took place in my sister's flat. I could get happily drunk and listen to music from the 70's and 80's.

So during this time, about August 2003, I was waiting to hear from the University about my loan. That worried me. I hadn't worked much in the last few years and so, naturally, I was skint! I had applied for the loan and there was no reason for the loans company or the university to turn me down. Still, I was worried and told myself that my dream wasn't going to become a reality because I wasn't going to get the loan. It made no difference to me that there was absolutely no evidence that this was the case. I was in the same position as everybody else. Waiting my turn. That's how my mind works. If there's nothing to concern myself with I'll find something to worry about.

I was accepted on the course I wanted to study, Media Writing. I had letters from the university informing me of term dates. However, I still hadn't heard from the loans company. Without the loan I couldn't go. It was the loan or nothing. I couldn't really prance or swagger with confidence, until I had written conformation that I was going to get a student loan. It was agonising. I was nearly there. When the letter arrived confirming I was getting the loan I danced in the kitchen. My dad hugged me and I felt great. There was the final proof that I, the 'black sheep' in the family, had finally made his dad proud. It seemed like my destiny had finally been put within reaching distance. That moment was special for me. At last I could look any member of my family in the eye. I could engage in any topic of conversation. I was actually going to make my family proud for the first time. I was a feeling that I'll never forget. It's what makes life worth living.

Paul Hill

Now I could start planning for the future again. I needed to buy pans and plates etc. My mother offered to come with me and buy some things I'd needed to take with me. My whole family, with the exception of my little sister, came out with me for drinks on my last night at home. It was a quiz night at one of the local pubs and I joked with my dad that we would come close to wining because they had a student on their team! However, this student was only good at answering really useless trivia questions.

My dad squeezed my stuff into the back of his car and we travelled together down to Southampton early Saturday morning. It's a long drive all that way. It was a sunny day, a nice day, and seen as I was looking for good omens I grabbed that tightly and held it as my own. We arrived at around three o'clock in the afternoon. When I was show my room I was staggered. Oh if omens really did mean anything I was surely onto a winner. It was a huge room, and it was all mine. It was twice the size of the average room in the halls. I was on the top floor and there were rooms on either side of the corridor. After my dad and I quickly dumped my gear into the room we went for a walk around Southampton city centre. I was really impressed with what I saw. There were loads of shops and lots of nice looking girls - it was my dad who offered that opinion. We bought the food and slowly walked back to my room in the halls.

At this point I was the only person in the halls. My dad was tired after the long drive. He told me he needed to sleep for a few hours. Rob let him borrow a mattress and we got a couple of hours kip. We went out that night. It was Saturday night and there were a lot of people about. I felt really good. I squeezed into some nice trousers. My dad and went out together and we had a good night. He said he really liked the look of the place and said he wished it were him that was going to be living there. I was sitting with my dad having a good time and genuinely happy with my place in the world and my prospects for the future.

The following morning, at around ten o'clock, I hugged my dad goodbye. He told he that he loved me and that he was proud of me. Just reliving those moments brings tears to my eyes. I watched him drive off and he gave me a brief wave. I stood in the basement car park and tried to cheer myself up. I felt sad because it had gone by so quickly. I felt really proud to be in my dad's company the past few days. It was a feeling that I desperately wanted to continue feeling.

CHAPTER TEN
UNIVERSITY

I arrived at Southampton Institute a week before the vast majority of students. I was one of the 'old codgers'. At the age of thirty, I was seen as a mature student. I was worried about being the oldest person in the whole of the university. It gave me something to worry about. The whole idea of me being there a week early was to refresh on my English and Maths and most importantly the thing that really caught my eye: advice on making notes in the lecture halls. Whilst I was in college, if I was sitting next to somebody and the teacher and the person next to me, while the teacher was talking, started to write something, I panicked. Was the person writing down something important? Should I be worried about why I hadn't seen fit to make a note of the same point? I wanted to have all the best possible advice and help available to me. It got to a point in college that I'd doodle just to feel that I wasn't missing out on anything!

The refresher course was called a 'Gateway Course'. I was really pleased to see so many people on it. I was even more pleased to note that I was one of the youngest people there. It was a real laugh. We got taught elemental mistakes that people make in English. We were shown around the library and issued with identification cards. At the end of the week, we had to stand up in groups and give a presentation on a certain theme. Our theme was the 'Electronic Library' and explain what it was and how to use it. Basically it consists of using the online data available and things like emails and useful websites were also involved. I cruised it. I've had to stand up and give speeches and presentations so many times in my life. At the end of the week the group went out together. Rather disappointingly, nobody really wanted to stay out. I was ready to party until late into the evening. We all stopped drinking at about five o'clock in the afternoon. I phoned my sister and said I wish she were with me to get drunk.

The following week was the start of 'freshers' week. This basically consists of all the new, first year students moving into halls, introductions to tutors and lecturer, more information about term times and dates and basically what the course entailed. The classes were huge. It became daunting when I saw just how many people were doing the same course. Each lecturer stood and told the classes about who they were. There was lots of nervous laughter about. At one stage it felt like I was in sitcom that relied on the canned laughter. There was a large fair in one of the council buildings in the city. It was like a trade fair where each stall was selling its products to new students. This was where the students could sign up for teams and individual pursuits for the year ahead. I was tempted to sign up to a football team and possibly even a rugby or American football team.

By this time I had met a few people from my halls. They were all stunned at the size of my room. It was fun looking at the reactions on their faces. I would joke and say things like 'you know what they say about a man with a big room?' My favourite was telling people that the room was so big that it had two different postcodes! It was really quite funny because even though in the halls, which held nearly three hundred people, there were loads of different faces and colours and shapes and sizes, the one thing that we all had in common was the 'lost' or 'rabbit caught in headlamp' look. In the first week and there was so much to take in including meeting new people and exploring various ways in which to get lost in the same place! It felt a little like when I started at Lyme Bay or Bod. There was a long corridor and there were loads of strange faces. I felt pretty daunted to be honest. This was a huge step for me. I had gone from living at home and feeling pretty average, to living in a building with nearly three hundred other people. I wanted to relax and enjoy the moment, but then that what people say after the moment has already passed.

The freshers week was carefully orchestrated to get the new students, the first years, into feeling more confident and making friends. As soon as I arrived, I said to my reflection in the mirror that I was going to do everything I could to make university work. I had worked bloody hard to get there. I wanted to enjoy and experience as much as could. I was like a man possessed. I had made some new friends and a couple of them, Alex and Phil, came out with me a few times on the pub crawls that the university had organised. The bonus about attending these events was that you were awarded with cheap beer and discounts to other clubs and bars. I would have loved to have gotten drunk and relaxed at this stage but I didn't know my new friends too well and I didn't really feel relaxed. There was plenty of time for fun later. I kept to my oath. I went out at every opportunity because I wanted to make a real go of it.

I lost a lot of weight and on the first Monday, I joined the gym. It was only a small gym but at least it was cheap and it opened until late every night. I was still very conscious about the way I looked. The month or so before I arrived at university I ran at least once every day, sometimes ran twice. However, when I enrolled on my course and was presented with all the documents and paperwork, passport photos were needed to prove identity. I didn't really want to have to do this because I still wasn't happy with who I was in the mirror. I got the photos and wasn't happy with how I looked. I stared long and hard at the four duplicate images of myself and really despised them. In retrospect, that wasn't good news. It meant that I was unhappy with myself and it also meant that it would have serious implications if things started to go wrong later on. I decided some drastic action was the order of the day. My hair was probably an inch longer than my ears. I decided to have a 'number one' which was not completely bald but the grade before that. I was happy with my image after the cut. I walked determinedly through Southampton city centre and did my best to calm myself down. I was still on edge and I was hoping to feel the elation I felt when I first arrived at Bodelwyydan.

I was like a keen boy scout. On my first proper day at university I was up early and ready to go much before 9 a.m. which was the time of the start of the first lecture. I was nervous, but even more determined. I sat next to be closest friend at university, Alex. He seemed amazed at the contents of my pencil case. Before the lecture began I opened up the pencil case and pulled out pens, markers, cello tape, correction fluid, rubbers and pencils, and best of all, a dicta phone. It must have looked like Mary Popins' bag. The idea of the dicta phone was to tape the lecture as an aide memoire. I was not the only person with this idea. Unfortunately, the recordings picked up not only the voice of the lecturer, but also picked every other sound. When I started my course in early October, there was a lot of coughing and sneezing going on, along with the squeaking of chairs. When I finished the lecture and played the tape in my room, I had to laugh. It was like a BBC sound effect album! I abandoned the idea very quickly after that.

I was delighted when I learned that the timetable was so flexible. I think I was only at the university for something like fourteen hours. I remember that Thursday was the longest day and Friday there were no classes at all! It was like having a long weekend! I was weight training twice a day when I first arrived. After my classes ended for the day I would go to the gym and use the running machine or the rower. I opted to use the rower because I would run at night as well. I was rowing twelve thousand metres each time I trained. This was taking me around fifty minutes to complete. Even at this stage I was a little concerned because despite the hard work I was putting in, I still didn't like what I saw in the mirror. My image drove me on to higher levels of determination. I wanted to look slimmer in the face and I wanted to fit easily into all my clothes. I was rushing a round like a lunatic because I wanted to look my best as soon as I could. You see I thought that if I was more comfortable with my reflection, then I would relax more. In retrospect, I had the same attitude whenever I worked away from home. It was true at Bodelwyddan and Lyme Bay, but as my depression worsened, it seemed not to matter. However, I was now at university and I would do anything and everything to make things work.

I phoned home a lot in the early stages. I was good to talk to my family. I would ask them about life at home and in return, with more than a hint of pride, I'd tell them about lectures, seminars and tutorials and how my attempts at cooking were going. I promised my mother that I would live on more than beans on toast while I was away. I was determined to stick to my word. Though, in all honesty, my food cupboard was full of beans and bread! I had plenty of milk and cheese in the fridge. Some of the people I met were really into complex dishes and I noted how long these dishes took to prepare. After the first few weeks, Alex let me try some of his special spaghetti bolognaise. I offered to make him something. Only thing that came to my mind was...beans on toast...with an egg! He declined my offer with a smile on his face.

The kitchen where I cooked and prepared my intricate, carefully planned beans on toast was called the blue kitchen. It quickly became the hub of activity because all the people that went on to be my friends always hung out in there. I think there were only about a dozen or so English students on my floor. There were loads of Spanish and Greeks and some Portuguese. Alex had loads of films on DVD and loads of people crammed into the blue kitchen to watch them. I was happier to listen to music.

I didn't miss a lesson for the first five weeks. My attendance was one of the best on the course. I continued to train hard but soon cut it down to once a day. When I first arrived, I went to the student union quite a few times. It was great in there because the drinks were cheap, as you'd expect, and at 5 – 6 p.m. and then again at 8 – 9 p.m. the union did a happy hour. Two drinks for the price of one! Brilliant! To get the most from this deal, you needed to drink as fast as you could. One time, I had six pints of cider in one hour! I enjoyed going there because it's what I always wanted. It was the student union - a place where only students of the university could go.

Though I did have some friends, I didn't really feel apart of a group. I have no idea why. I was looking pretty sharp and I would have loved to have found a girlfriend or...let's be honest, I would have liked to have had sex. I was getting a little down because I wanted girls to fancy me and take notice of me. I went to a few parties, one of which was to celebrate handing in our first assignment. I had worked really hard and I needed to relax. I went to this party, which was taking place in the blue kitchen. I went to the gym first and I had even brought some new music. I wanted to get drunk so I could relax. I was uptight because

I wasn't really enjoying my experience too much. By this time I was having to continually tell myself that I could make it and that I did believe and have faith in myself. I asked a lot of these questions while in lectures or seminars. I'd be trying to concentrate and listen to the lecturer and in the back of my mind I kept asking myself 'did I really have enough faith to survive at university?' 'Did I really, honestly believe that I had any kind of future?' It was horrible and very distracting. Sadly and very worryingly, my reply was always 'yes I could make it and I did have faith'. It wasn't convincing me at the time. I needed to be strong and at that time, so early on, I knew I was beginning to sink into depression.

At this party, since it was Halloween at the time, some people got dressed up. The atmosphere was happy and relaxed and thankfully, they were playing music from the 60's 70's 80's. There were a lot of younger people who wanted to listen to modern music, which I think is abysmal! I tried to relax and let myself go. Other people were getting drunk and looked happy so why couldn't I? At this point, I was looking for some positive reinforcement. I needed to find faith and confidence from somewhere. I wanted to hear or feel that I was getting some attention from somebody. It's hard to explain. I was asking questions of myself and I needed to respond. The best and most likely way was to have a really good night and show this doubting thought that I could make it. To have a pretty girl look at me would mean that all my training and hard work in the gym was paying off. I was desperately trying to be happy.

No luck. I trundled off on my own and sulked in my room. It wasn't the night I needed or hoped for. I can see on reflection that I was putting far too much pressure on myself at a very early stage in my new life. I needed to do something positive and do it quickly. What hurt even more was that I had received a really good result in my 'script and performance' lecture. I received a first, which was the top mark. I should have been elated with that. I thanked Seamus, my lecturer. I honestly felt that I had received the mark because he felt sorry for me! I was in trouble and I knew it. The only door open to me was to visit one of the universities councillors.

I set up an appointment and I immediately felt a little better about the world. At least I had done the right thing. I needed to respond and I had definitely done something positive. During this period I continued to train hard. It was important to me to feel like I was getting something right. Ironically my performances were not as bad as I perhaps make out. After the fifth week I had missed one lecture and that was because I was kept awake 'til four in the morning. Claire, my councillor was a lovely person. Really warm and easy to talk to. She thanked me for coming to see her when I did. I told her a little about my history and my fears and that I felt I was losing control. She told me that it was good that I was there because I was trying to do something about the situation before it got out of hand. I told my family that I was seeing the 'shrink' because things were becoming a little frayed around the edges. They were all really supportive of me. I think they appreciated that I was honest with them and that I was doing the right thing. I didn't tell any of my close friends at University because, at that time, I didn't really have any.

I can't remember how many times I went to see Claire, but it wasn't that many. It was important to be able to talk to somebody and not expect either sympathy or the feeling that the person you've told thinks you're crazy. At about the same time, I made another positive move. I had been thinking about getting a job for a while. I needed to manage my finances properly and I didn't want to spend my entire student loan on alcohol like a hell of a lot of other people do. One of my more casual friends, Steve, told me about a vacancy in a pub called the Osbourne. It was a half hour walk from my halls. To be honest, I could have gone for any job. I mean that there were loads of jobs that students could do. I felt like I needed to prove that I could handle anything thrown at me. Through experience I knew that once I had started to doubt and question myself, I usually end up hiding away and confining myself to my room. I didn't have the option while I was at university. I still had to go to lectures and seminars. I had a brief interview with the landlord and I managed to avoid admitting that I was awful at pouring a pint. He took my on there and then. It was a Tuesday and my job was to work on Sunday and Monday evenings from eight until twelve. As I walked back to my halls, I was quietly optimistic about the future. I had got myself a job and I was seeing a councillor.

It was getting harder and harder to keep these negative thoughts at bay. I was trying to concentrate and pay as much attention as I needed while I was sitting in lectures. I was trying to listen to the lecturers rather than the doubts in my head. I was still going out and trying to have fun in the blue kitchen. I got jealous because I felt that I wasn't really fitting in as smoothly as everybody else was. In an attempt to try and 'steady the ship,' I was training twice a day again. I hated the person in the mirror as I watched myself rowing for fifty minutes! As I write this now, I'm really impressed with the fact that I could row for so long. I was so fit, but I was angry and frustrated. The more I trained and continued to feel low, the more I began to fear that history was about to repeat itself.

I was pretty average behind the bar in the Osbourne. I'm polite and well mannered and when I need to be social I can be. I hoped that before the customer would drink their pint that I'd poured, they'd become distracted and look away, then drink the pint before actually thought about what they were drinking. As my confidence was pretty low, I thought that I was the worst barman on earth. Nobody actually said anything like that, but I was on a slippery slope by that point and I couldn't see the good in anything I did. Despite the fact that I had gotten myself a job and I was talking to a shrink, I still was struggling. To be honest, I've seen a lot of 'shrinks' in my time and none of them ever made me feel as calm as Claire did. When I was with her I felt sure she understood exactly what I was saying. She made the right responses and I calmed down. When the session finished and I was walking back to my halls, I felt weakened and lost. I needed to be in her company as long as possible.

Around this time, in a subject called 'Writing the Culture,' I was a part of a group who had to do a presentation. My part of the presentation focused on the famous American boxer Jack Johnson. He was the first black heavyweight champion of the world. I had worked hard on my part. I had informed all my lecturers that I was suffering, possibly with depression. The presentation should have lasted 15 minutes. Ours went on for over twenty. The lecturer was critical of our performance. Sadly, he targeted me. He asked me why I had decided to choose boxing to show culture in the 1900's. I didn't have the strength or the confidence to fight back as Jack Johnson would have done. I had chosen boxing because it empowered black people at that time, especially in the States. I was devastated. I told him the day before that I was struggling with depression and he seemed quite sympathetic. My point was that a black boxer had beaten a white man in a fair fight. This empowered the blacks and the many white government officials were worried about this. That was the cultural link.

I hated the lecturer for doing that. Maybe he was right, but he could have talked to me on my own. I asked Alex to wait for me, because I, like the rest of the group were being given our mark for the presentation. We were given a 2-2. I walked home with Alex and he told me I was overreacting. I had taken him into my confidence and told him I was suffering from depression. At the time I wanted him to say something to make feel better. I don't mean I expected praise or a compliment. I just expected him to help somehow. I was panicking and I phoned Claire. She told me I could see her. When I did, she was brilliant. She ordered me to sit down and breathe deeply. I then told her what had happened. She calmed me down and said the right things. I can't remember what they were but I left feeling better. She suggested that I see the course leader and explain to her the troubles I was having.

A meeting was arranged with the course leader in one of the councillor's offices. By now, despite my best efforts, I was feeling low. I was doing all the usual things I do when I feel threatened. I was running and rowing, but I wasn't getting any enjoyment from these activities. I was doing them because I wanted to prove to myself that things were going wrong, but I still had the faith in myself to train. The meeting went a lot better than I hoped for. I told the course leader that my work was being affected by my constantly low mood. I was finding concentration and motivation very hard. Perhaps the most pertinent point I made was the fact that I was scared that I was going loose my place on the course because my attendance, which at this point was starting to flag, wasn't good enough. It turned out that the course leader also suffered from depression. She insisted that I not worry and told me that she would talk to the other lecturers and made it clear to me that if I didn't show up for my lectures, all lecturers would know why. Also, when it came to marking my work, the lecturers would bear in mind that I was suffering and perhaps, their marks would reflect that. At the end of the meeting, when the course leader had left, I hugged Claire, as I always did, at the end of the sessions. I felt much better and a lot of the pressure had been lifted off my shoulders. I was able to hand the assignments in on time and I felt more relaxed.

Life wasn't so bad for the week or so after that. Things were never the same again though. I mean, all the excitement of the earlier days was gone, and now matter how much I tried to 'showboat', I knew I had a real struggle on my hands. There were two possible saviours on the horizon. Firstly, it was around middle to late November. By 19th December, the Christmas Holiday period started. All students had three weeks off. I was looking forward to going home for a while. The second thing was that my sister was coming down to see me. As she used to work in Portsmouth, and she had lots of friends there. She was visiting her new boyfriend, Lee. I was really looking forward to seeing her. I took quite a while deciding what I was going to wear! That was a good sign. In meant I was not thinking solely about doom and gloom. I walked to the pub where I had arranged to meet my sister. As I walked through the chilly city centre and passed all the people running around and panicking about Christmas, I felt pretty good about myself for a change. I wanted to tell my sister how I'd been feeling and what I'd gone through. I needed to tell her. Also, a few months before, she told me of her pregnancy and I wanted to hug her and tell her how proud I was of her.

I got to the pub first and bought myself a pint. I was happy and nervous. I don't know why I felt nervous. I had nothing to feel nervous about. I sat in the pub and waited, and while I did I reflected on what I had told Claire earlier in the day. Whenever I was with Claire and I told her how worried I was and that I doubted myself and my chances of finishing the course, she always made me feel so much better. She had a lovely soft voice and I think that alone helped soothed me. What worried me was I only felt stronger and felt that I could find the belief that I needed when I was in her presence. When I was on my own, my thoughts would fill in any silences with overwhelming negative thoughts. The irony was, these thoughts were posed as questions. Did I really believe I could make it? Did I see any kind of future? If things were going so well why did I need a councillor and why did I need to see the course leader? Now, I can see that I already knew the answers to these questions. It was horrible to have to experience this. I needed the to be confident in myself, but it wasn't there.

When my sister finally arrived she was late! I was in for a disappointment. I thought she would be alone. I had a lot to tell her and I wanted to talk to her in private. She walked in with her new boyfriend, and though I know Lee really well now and I know he's a really good bloke and of course, the father of my sister's baby, at that moment, I wished he wasn't there. I hoped it didn't show on my face. We had a quick drink in that pub and then we moved off to somewhere else. I had envisaged getting nicely, sensibly drunk with my elder sister. But neither my sister nor Lee were drinking pints. I felt awful. I had only just met them and I wanted to go. I think we went to a few pubs and we decided to split. I hugged my sister and told her I would see her at home for Christmas. I shook Lee's hand and told him it was nice meeting him. I was angry with myself for being so rude. I made my way very slowly back to my halls. I think I had told myself before the meeting with my sister that I would feel much better after seeing her. I had made the meeting out to be far too important, and consequently the disappointment was much greater. I don't think it made that much difference with Lee being there. People suffering with depression tend to over exaggerate to huge effects. I felt so low because I was expecting to feel so much more positive after meeting my sister. I wanted to use the meeting as a springboard to finishing off my work before going home for the holiday period. I tried to phone Claire and tell her what had happened. She was no longer at the office because it was six-thirty in the evening. I passed all the Christmas shoppers and remembered to laugh and smile because it was that time of year.

It was the day after I met my sister that I was supposed to be working a shift at the pub. I was a Sunday evening shift and my start time was eight o'clock. I remember sitting in my bed, trying to rouse myself into some kind of direction. I didn't feel like going in to work. I had only been there for three weeks and already I was at the point of letting them down. I phoned up the number and I had the worse possible start. My boss answered, and in the background I could hear lots of laughter and raised voices. It was the time of the Rugby World Cup. All pubs were very busy and ours was no exception. I would have been better for me if one of the other staff had answered the phone. My boss was out of breath and he had to ask me to speak up because of all the noise in the pub. I told him I was feeling unwell and that I was sorry, but I couldn't work my shift that night. I told him I would let him know if I could work the Monday or not. His attitude was that of a lover, jilted by his wife to be. He asked me if I was serious and did I realise how busy they were at the moment. I apologised again and hopefully, with not too much sarcasm, I told him it was not my intention to be ill at that moment. He thanked me, but I gathered it wasn't authentic appreciation. He sounded angry and let down. I felt awful. It wasn't like I was planning a huge orgy or preparing to go out on an 'bender'. I didn't set foot out of my room all day. I went to my lectures and seminars on Monday and I also got a session with Claire. I told her what had happened with meeting my sister and I also told her of my phone call to my boss. I cannot remember what she said, but I must have done me some good. The session ended with me promising her that I would consider going to work in the evening. I think we agreed that if I did, I would feel like at least something was going right.

I went to work that night. I knew that the landlord was really unhappy that I hadn't turned in the previous night, but what could I do? I walked into the pub with all the fluidity of robot. I was determined to get the showdown over and done with in the quickest possible time. For the day or so I had been under deluge of scenarios in my mind. I always see the negative in everything. I already told myself that I was going to be sacked because I was an awful barman and I'd let the pub manager down. With all the pressures starting to accumulate on my shoulders and in my mind, remaining calm and sensible was like asking me to explain the practical uses of algebra….. impossible!

My landlord was disappointed with me but he wasn't as angry as I thought he might be. He explained that he had to work from seven in the morning until twelve in the evening. He wasn't happy, but at least I had phoned up. The real problem was with the assistant manager, Ian. I never liked him as soon as I met him. I didn't like the way he spoke to me or the way he spoke to others. He was really sarcastic towards me. Rather than admitting that I was suffering with depression, I told them I had a problem with my insulin. The landlord seemed appeased but Ian, like a smug little worm, made comment after comment about how I had let the staff down and how he, however ill he was, always came to work.

From talking with Claire, the plan was that working in the pub that evening would make me feel much better about myself. It was supposed to give me more self-respect and confidence. As I plodded home (I write 'plodded' because all the bounce and swagger had gone), I felt even more deflated. I didn't like being out of my room and my confidence was low. How a person walks is often an indication of how they see themselves, unless they have an injury or something. As I made my way home, I was thinking about going home for the holidays. I had wanted my return home to be a celebration. I could walk home proudly and tell my family what university was like, and what was my room like. At that moment, I really didn't want to go home. I can't say why for sure, but I had no pride in myself and I didn't want my family to have to see it for themselves.

I must have revived because a week before the holiday period started, I bought a ticket from the train station. I also bought some new music and the same night, there was a party taking place in the blue kitchen. I thought that if I could have fun at this party, then I would be in good spirits for the brief time I remained at university. I'd seen Claire a few more times since then and I was still training really hard. I was desperate to forget my melancholy and try and have some fun. Everybody was in high spirits because most of the students in the halls were going home for Christmas. I had to pretend to be as excited by the same prospect. It was no good. I knew that my work was being affected by my mood. The laughter and the jokes and singing, they seemed to infect everybody except me. The kitchen was crammed full of people, yet I seemed to be on my own. I tried to make conversation, but when your mind is so intent on telling you that you've 'blown it', that even at university you mess things up, it's impossible to listen, let alone talk to people. At times like these, faking the smiles and the laughter is so painful.

A few days before I was scheduled to leave and go home, I had another session with Claire. This was the final straw for me. She told me because of the holiday period, we were not going to be able to meet for about a month. I had decided before this meeting that I couldn't go home. I couldn't face my family and pretend that I was happy and that everything was okay. I had hoped to stay where I was and continue seeing Claire. Her news absolutely blew me away. I'm not blaming her. She had family and friends that she wanted to be around at Christmas. It just left me feeling totally alone.

Paul Hill

When I told her of my plans, she told me that she disagreed with them. However, she gave me the number of a local psychiatrist and told me I could set up some sessions there if I felt in danger of harming myself. She hugged me and told me, very confidently, that she would see me in the New Year and that everything would turn out okay. I never saw again.

That night, I think it was a Thursday evening; I reached a new pitifully low tide. I didn't want to have to make the phone call to my mother. I had left it until a day before I was meant to go home to tell my parents I had changed my mind. I hated myself. I texted my dad and told him the situation. How weak and cowardly is that? I didn't even have the courage or the decency to speak to him. He phoned me back straight away and told me that my mother had been crying. She was worried and really upset. Did I have any idea what I had done to her? By this time, I was falling deeper and deeper into despair. My mother phoned me and asked why? I told her that I couldn't face anybody. I felt awful. The night before, despite the fact that I trained in the gym for over an hour, I returned to my room feeling as low as I possibly could. The halls were almost vibrating with excitement and energy. People, even me, had worked really hard and deserved a break. The laughter and buzz of adrenaline were impossible to avoid.

At this point, I wasn't sure if I was going home or not. I told Claire that I wouldn't, but I wasn't so sure. I don't know why I did what I did, but it's too late now. In bed, the night before I made the text to my dad telling him I wasn't going home, I started to feel the fat I had on my stomach. I was curled up, lay the foetal position, and so there was more fat than usual. I felt all my training was for nothing. I was fat and useless and I had nothing to live for. I was like the time I was in Portsmouth and I was sitting around the table. It was an onslaught initiated by my own mind. I went down to

178

the chocolate machine and spent a small fortune. I plodded again back to my room and I felt like I was walking to the tune if the death march. I knew if I ate those chocolates there was no way I was going home. I ate them and have regretted it ever since.

Over the two weeks I got worse and worse. I went out to the local supermarket and bought loads of cakes and sweets etc. I watched my weight balloon and felt like I was watching all this happen to somebody else. Because nobody, apart from one lad, was left in my section of the halls, it wasn't so bad. I hated myself for being so weak. Wasn't this my big chance? Wasn't I going to make my parents and the rest of my family proud? I felt abused and beaten. I continued to put on the weight and hate myself and my reflection. I was on a downhill spiral. I had stopped using the gym and didn't run either. I went to see a woman who wanted to assess me and see if I needed a psychiatrist. She told me she'd set up a meeting as soon as she could. It was only a few days later. I saw this woman in a mental ward. I hate to sound so crude, but that's what it was. I was asked if I wanted to stay for a while? It was not a nice place to be. One person was running around in a circle and another one was trying to protect his medicine from me. I was hoping for a quiet room, a place where I could read. I declined and told them I would be okay as long as I could talk to somebody. The woman assured me I would speak to the psychiatrist in a matter of days.

All this eating of cakes and sweets resulted in me having to go to the dentist and have a couple of teeth pulled out. By that time, it felt like I existed on autopilot. I ate and read and slept, but I didn't really experience these things. I was anxious about having to go back for the new term. I felt a mess, but I looked even worse. Not even the BBC special effects department could replicate the way I looked. I saw the psychiatrist and at least he gave me some good news. He said he could help me and that he was prepared to work with me. Not so great when it meant that I would have to remain at university and, of course, that meant facing everyone again looking the way I looked. I thanked him and told him I would see him for the next appointment. I didn't see him again either.

I had been keeping in touch, via the phone, with my parents. They knew how I was feeling and that I had reached rock bottom…. again. To be honest, I was relieved when my dad phoned me up and told me he would come and pick me up and he also advised me to have some time off and return the following year. I was very grateful to hear those words. He told me he would leave it until the start of the forthcoming week. It was the 22nd December when my dad phoned. If he didn't pick me up within the next two days, I'd be forced to face loads of students because many were coming back to the halls before New Years Eve. My dad agreed to pick me up the next day. I have said many things about my dad, but I love him more than words can say. We had an awful start, but I have so much to thank him for.

The following day, at about eleven in the morning, I awoke to my phone going off. I answered it and my dad said. 'Let me in, kid'. He was waiting at the front door, at the entrance to the halls! I was shocked. I hadn't even started getting my things together. He gave me a hug and we started to pack my things and load them into the car. When it was done, he had some toast and a cup of tea. He told me that we'd leave early the next morning. I wanted to go then. He explained it was a long drive and he was not going to make the return journey in the same day. We went out that night and he told me things would get better and I'd be back in a year anyway. I nodded my head in agreement but kept my mouth closed and my thoughts to myself. Oddly enough, my dad had a really good night. I couldn't get the thought out of my mind that only a few months before, I had been out drinking with my dad in Southampton and looking forward to my future. How cruel life is. I was going home because yet again I had failed. Where could I go now and how could I ever take pride in myself again?

We left at about nine the next morning. It was New Years Eve. I felt incredibly alone and adrift and floating down a stream in no particular direction. I wanted to cry. My dream, the one that I had clung to for so long was over. I was hurting so much and at the same time trying to convince myself and my dad that I'd return to Southampton the following term, or the following year. I've not set foot in Southampton since.

CHAPTER ELEVEN
RETURN FROM
UNIVERSITY

It takes along time to drive from Southampton to Nottingham. All the way home I couldn't get the thought out of my head that I was the same person, who only a few months before, had, perhaps for the first time, seen pride in his parents' eyes. My thoughts were so vicious. I kept thinking about my dad and me, on my first night in Southampton. How, when I said goodbye to him, I was determined to make him, and the rest of my family proud of me. All the nice people I had met and how proud I was of myself. What happened to it? Where did it go and why did I allow it to leave me? I think people who suffer with depression never find solace or support. What they find, amongst their thoughts, are accusations and recriminations. No support. I needed, at that point, to believe that I had done all I could in the circumstances. I wrote to my tutor and told him what had happened. I told him that I had been seeing a 'shrink'. I asked that I be given time off in order to become 'sane' again. I would return to my studies when I felt that I could give all I had to offer.

I received a letter a few weeks later telling me that I would be given a year and then I could return. So, you see, I had nothing to be ashamed of. I had done everything I needed to do in order to return. When I arrived home, I paused before walking through our front door. I forced myself through the door. My mother, elder sister and Lee, her boyfriend, were all in the posh room. What I love about my family is the fact that we are all very down to earth. They knew I felt... there are no words to describe how I felt. I walked in and it was if I'd just returned from going to the local shop to get a pint of milk. They made no big deal of my return and I loved them for it. My mother told me that all would be okay. I hugged my sister and made polite talk and called my sister various names that referred to her being fat: she was three or four months pregnant at this stage.

It was New Years Eve and Lee and my sister left at around 8 o'clock. I felt more relaxed because I wouldn't have to face any of my old friends. At this stage I had a beard and I had put on quite a lot of weight. I was glad to be in an environment where I didn't have to pretend that I was happy or content with life. I had several bottles of cider in the car and I had brought them in with me. From about 7 o'clock onwards I had started to drink. It's nice to be able to stand up and face the New Year. I don't know why, but as the night went on, I actually felt quite good about the coming year. My mum was in the front room with my dad and I popped in and out all night. I continued drinking and by the time the count down came, I was alright. Not happy nor looking forward, but I wasn't desperate or sad. I was in the middle somewhere. My dad stayed up with me until about one in the morning. I went to bed and I continued drinking. I used my mum's Walkman and I must admit, I was happily drunk whilst listening to music. I don't know what time it was, but it was around 2 o'clock in the morning when my dad came into my room and pointed out that my singing had awoken him and my mum. I was sorry and not long afterwards, I fell asleep. The following day, when eating a lunch my mum had prepared, my dad recounted the story of my singing the previous night. My sister and Lee were also eating. My dad included that when he came into my room, so early in the morning, not only was I singing in a very offkey tone, I was also 'air guitaring' as well!

I needed some kind of plan. What was I going to do now? I went to see my doctor and almost had an argument with him. I told him what had happened and what my plans for the year were. I wanted, for the time being, to claim incapacity benefit which meant I wasn't able to actively seek work. He basically accused me of abandoning university because I hadn't made any friends. He obviously got the wrong end of the stick. We cleared that up and I told him I did planned to return to my studies. I wanted to return, but even back then, months ago, I didn't really believe that I would. My dream had become tainted. I honestly thought that once I was at university, I would not be troubled or affected by depression because studying is what I always wanted. The fact that I had failed there, like I failed pretty much everywhere else, meant that I would never look at university in the same way again.

The fact that university was no longer the beacon or the 'shimmering light' it had once been left me feeling isolated. Part of me wanted to go back to Uni. I hadn't actually failed, I ran into some problems and was given a period of time to get the problems sorted. Deep in my heart, though, I didn't really believe that I would go back, and I think that spelt the end of that chapter of my life, and the end of a dream.

It felt odd being back home. I was so proud when left and yet here I was, repeating the same mistakes and feeling pretty much the same way I always felt. I don't remember how long it was until I decided I should get a job. When things are really bad, I mean when I first came home from the university, I remember telling my dad that all I wanted to do was stay in my room and read. Reading always relaxes me. It takes me away from who I am and I become so involved with the story that I can, for a very short while, feel like I am as normal as every other person. This means, sadly, that I rarely set foot out of the house. When I first arrived home, I tried getting back in shape and running again. I had, though not by any means a firm plan of trying to recover and get my head back in order. My doctor told me that the waiting list to see a Clinical Psychologist was very long. He didn't seem too hopeful and I didn't really believe that I would ever get to see one.

I have no disrespect to the counselling profession. Counsellors sit and listen and you can get a lot of bad thoughts and feelings off your chest. However, I've always been under the impression that Psychologists and Psychiatrists are people the can actually construct and formulate a plan of action. I've seen a lot - too many counsellors and I know they can help. I wanted the best help I possibly could and that meant a Clinical Psychologist. So, as far as I was concerned, I was just going to have to wait and see if I could talk to a Clinical Psychologist. I found running and exercising very difficult. However depressed and low I felt previously, I always knew that if I hung in there and fought, I was smart enough to get myself to university. It used to spur me on, to ignite and motivate me. From the moment I returned home, the dream that had seen and steered me through some really nasty waters was gone forever. I found it really difficult to run because there was nowhere I was running to. I just seem to be running away.

I do not know the exact date that I retuned to work. Sometimes, when I've been off for a long time, I feel I need to get out of my 'safe' environment. I suppose that's part of the problem. I really did need to feel safe and secure and my old room offered me that comfort. It's like a security blanket.

I used the comforting vibes of my room to soothe some of the pain that I was feeling from my pathetic attempt at university. The 'safety' and 'comfort' provided by that kind of environment actually develops into a kind of smothering and suffocation of all other activities. Nothing else matters as long as I could retreat the safety of my room. I suppose it casts a distortion on how real life is. I needed to break the spell. I rarely left the room but my mind had set sail on a different course. As well as my love for reading, I have also written many, not yet completed short stories. I have also written 60 pages of a script, which is based roughly on my best friend in Wales, Ian, and another fictitious character. I have also written short stories that have been completed.

Throughout my life, people have told me that these are good and I should consider trying to get them published. Lovely to hear that kind of thing. However, I believe one of the many problems that depression afflicts on the sufferer is that you don't believe it's you they're talking about. It happened at university. My lecturer in 'Script and Performance' told me the reason the group I was working with were awarded top marks was because of my efforts. I thanked him and wondered if he realised it was me he was talking to! I would be complimented on my writing, and these positive remarks would all too quickly be replaced by my own 'You're useless and you know it'. Time and time again, these thoughts dominate my mind like a pack of shaven headed football hooligans. What I wanted all along, even at university, was to be able to write for a living. For me to have my work published would help greatly in fighting the demons that have been taunting me ever since I left university. My plan was to try and find an agent who would help me get published. I had Internet access so I knew it wasn't going to be a problem researching. For the moment I was living again. I felt more positive and I remember telling my parents of my plans.

At the same time as looking for an agent, I signed up at an employment agency and within one day of signing up, I was offered a job. Fortunately, the place I was working was called Colwick. It's only fifteen minutes on bike and it's down hill all the way there (unfortunately that means it was uphill all the way back!). I really liked working there. It was a warehouse and my job was to put stick away in its proper location. Once this is done, the people employed as 'pickers' would refer to their list, and pick the stock up. I enjoyed my job because it entailed loads of walking and lots and solitary work. I made a few decent mates and it wasn't long before I was telling people I was taking a break from university. It was technically true, if only I believed it myself. I felt, for the first time in a long time, free from pressure of any kind. The pay was poor, £4.50 an hour. Still, it was like therapy to me. I enjoyed the exercise because I needed to lose some weight. I was running again in the evening. I still felt pretty low, but at least I had a job that I enjoyed and I had, by the second week of my stay there, found an agent who liked my work.

Trolling through the Internet I found the name of a highly recommend literary agent by the name of Darin Jewell who runs The Inspira Group Literary Agency. I sent him the first three chapters of a children's story that I had been working on and off for a few years. I didn't expect to hear anything but I was emailed back and told by Darin that he thought my story was good and he might be able to help get it published. I cannot explain how good I felt about life after reading that. My mind was flooded with Oscar ceremonies and award acceptance speeches. I can't help it. Everything is either absolutely wonderful or it's utterly dreadful. There's no in-between with me. That is something that a councillor once told me as well. I tried to remain clam and focused as I told my parents the news, but awards and book signings were getting in the way of how I constructed my speech. I was excited. It was like a kiss of life to me. Over the next few weeks, I was sent a literary contract and I was quite cocky at work. I didn't get too carried away though. I still had the thought asking me if I was caught in one of those fantasies again. Did I really think this was going to work?

Sadly I was starting to have problems at work. Nothing to do with being down or depressed. I was having really bad problems with my teeth. I was having regular toothaches and they were causing me to leave work early or sometimes, not going into work at all. One day I apologised to my boss, Mark, and told him I was going to have to get some painkillers. He looked really annoyed and told me he was getting sick of me having so much time off. I would have loved to have stayed and argued with him but I was in too much pain. I went to the nearest chemist and bought the strongest painkillers I could find. I went home and fell asleep. The following day and got an emergency dental appointment. They extracted the offending tooth, and by 11'clock I had arrived at work. As I walked through the building and passed some of my work colleagues, I knew something wasn't right. I found my boss mark and before I could give him the good news about my tooth, he told me that I had been sacked, but said I could work for the remainder of the day if I wished. I felt stunned, but not too down. I was expecting something like this to happen. I had missed a lot of work.

It was roughly around this time that Darin, my agent, I told me that he submitted my work to a list of publishers. I was awaiting their comments with incredible reluctance. As long as there was a chance I might get published, life was more bearable. At the same time in our house, there was buzz of excitement and anticipation. My elder sister was heavily pregnant and my younger sister, who lived in Canterbury, was also pregnant. Our house was a very happy environment. Lee came up to stay a lot and of course the topic of conversation was all about the baby or babies, if you include my little sister as well. I was as happy as I could be for them. I found it really difficult because my mum and dad were clearly very proud of their daughters and they were looking forward to being grandparents. I kept asking myself would I make my mum and dad feel that way? At that time I was struggling to get some kind of positive spin on life. To make things worse, the story I had written that Darin had submitted to the publishing houses was not getting placed. He also told me that the genre in which I was trying to become published was oversubscribed at the moment. My story was a children's fantasy, and Harry Potter seemed to have a corner on the market. I knew there was a reason that I didn't like those books!

So I was back to feeling the way I usually felt - alone and insecure. I was unhappy because of my books nose diving and the atmosphere in the house was far too happy for me! For the first time, I started thinking in terms of moving out and getting my own place. This, of course, would mean that I needed a steady income. Before I made this decision, however, Darin phoned and offered me some good advice. He told me that I could write well and that I needed a break, which he said would come. In order to become published I needed to write something that would appeal to the market to get published. I know that sounds obvious. He asked me, because he's a decent bloke and I confided in him that I had problems with depression, what I thought about writing about my experiences with depression. I felt, at the time, I didn't really have much to write about. Darin gave me a rough outline of what kind of chapters I should consider. At first, I didn't like the idea. I couldn't see me being able to sustain an 'interesting' view on depression. Darin told me to think about it. He asked me to submit a chapter outline with a brief about what each chapter would contain. I couldn't do it. I was depressed and down and I decided I couldn't do it.

Finally, I found some inspiration. When I thought about all my experiences, all that I'd been through, I changed my mind. I submitted eight chapters to my agent and sat back and waited. I was still pretty miserable at this time. was also anxious about what was going to happen next in my life. I was angry with myself because both my sisters' were making my parents so proud. All I could do was think of how I had let them down when I returned from Southampton. I needed to get out of the house and I needed another job, and I got another job about thirty minutes from where I lived. This time I was cleaning clutch plates and clutch covers. I'm not a driver so I had never seen a clutch before. As soon as I got there I didn't like the job. However, if I was going to move out and get my own pad, I needed money. I wasn't depressed when I arrived, but nor was I comfortable with myself. I believed, somewhere within myself, that there was a possibility that I could write something about my experience with depression. At the time I started work at this latest job, I was on top of those my depressive thoughts. They were still in my head, but I tried hard to ignore them. The immediate future for me was earning enough money to move into my own place and focus on what I was going to put in the book. Those thoughts were taking dominance in my mind.

I think to be honest with myself, another reason I wanted to move out of home was because I was finding it hard to be able to look at any member of my family in the eye. I cannot explain how devastating it was to have returned early from university. I felt no pride in myself and felt like every time I opened my mouth, I had no right to speak, no right to air my views because, yet again, I had let myself and everyone else down. I loved being in the limelight before I went to university, but when I arrived home I felt I had nothing to offer. Another, more practical reason to go was because my sister had moved out of her flat and back home. It's hard to do justice to how I was feeling. I felt like I didn't belong to my family. I had let them down again and it was so painful to have to face them and pretend that all was fine and that I was on my way back. It certainly didn't feel like I was on my way back.

After a few weeks of working at my present job, I found a place and paid my months rent in advance. The house was about twenty minutes from where I lived at present. There were two other occupants and we all shared the kitchen, lounge and bathroom. It was sixty-five pounds rent a week. It wasn't too fussed because I was working at the time. I was almost excited at the thought of moving. Despite the fact that I was now starting to write my book, I was still very worried about the future. So many things had gone wrong before. Why should this time be any different? I had no faith in my future. My parents were all for the move. My dad, as always, helped me pack my stuff and drove it to my new home. I moved in on a Saturday towards the end of June 2004. It didn't take long for me to unpack because I do not have many things. I had an upstairs room and it was quite big. I wanted to feel more elated and excited about this. It was a huge step for me, but I couldn't let go of the past. I was expecting something to go wrong so I was very cautious with how I was feeling.

Work was starting to become a problem for me, yet again. Some places, like the last place I worked at, you like instantly. It's a combination of the job and the people you work with. I hated this new job from day one and hated myself for having to pretend that I liked those I worked with. Despite the fact that I was making positive strides forward, I was starting to struggle. My own mind, for some reason, continued to taunt me with questions like 'how were my friends getting along at university?' Do you think when they graduate they'll be working in a job like this?' I know now, as I write these accounts, that I'm destroying my own chances in life. I can see that. I wanted to scream at the top of my lungs that I was sick of these destructive thoughts! Why did I persecute myself? One lad, Darren, on more than one occasion told me to cheer up. He told me that I had a miserable face all the time. When you feel so unstable inside, it's very hard to continue to smile. A really bad sign for me was the fact that I was increasingly looking forward to the weekends. Not because I had anything planned, but because I hated working at the place. I was sick of these thoughts in my head tormenting me.

I continued to try my best. I wasn't very good at the job, but I put a lot of that down to my mental state. One Wednesday afternoon, at around four-thirty in the afternoon, my supervisor, Jamie, called me into the office. I definitely walked with the 'death march' tune in my mind. Waiting for me in the office was Jamie and Graham, the manager of the section where I was working. Graham told me that he was a little concerned that I wasn't at the stage that I needed to be. I was on trial and I was being assessed. Jamie stuck the boot in further saying something about me still having a lot to learn and it wasn't looking likely that I would be offered a full-time job. I knew, even as I told my bosses that I could and would improve, that I was going to quit. I said goodbye and told them both that I'd see them in the morning. I never saw either of them again.

I rode home and I felt numb. I recognised this feeling by now. I was about too quit yet another job. That night, I got very little sleep. I was still having this tremendous battle in my head. I wanted to quit. I felt empty and I felt that I could no longer force myself to go to work. That's what I'd been doing. Agonising each morning whether or not to turn up. Like so many times before, I felt empty and devoid of any energy. In a state of panic, I lay in my bed and attempted to see some sort of future for myself.

I hated working where I was working. I hated my refection in the mirror. I phoned up the agency and informed them that I was unwell. The following morning, very early, so I only got the answer machine, I phoned up the agency again and this time told them the truth - I was suffering from depression and I could no longer cope. For the next few days, I hardly moved from my bed. I immersed myself in books. Words and stories helped me forget who I was and what my present problems were.

Within a few days I had informed the council and I was, again, on sickness benefit. My real concern was how was I going to pay the rent? I needed to apply to the council again. It's very difficult having to fill in forms at the best of times, but when you're feeling incredibly adrift of the rest of humanity, it's even harder. I knew that once the forms were complete that I would have a long wait. The next months rent, I think that was August, I could pay, through my own savings, but after that? I would have to tell my landlord and hope he was flexible. My doctor had informed me that I would only have to wait a few months before I saw a Clinical Psychologist. I think the reason that I had 'jumped' the queue was because of the accumulative affect of all my 'sick notes' and pleas to my doctor. Though it wasn't something to look forward to, it was something other than sadness or negativity.

At roughly the same time as my latest crisis, my elder sister gave birth to Morgan Rhianna, her baby daughter. My mother and father were proud and delighted. I had, only a few days before, told them I had quit work and I was on benefits again. They didn't seem surprised. My initial reaction to my sister's daughter being born was happiness, but it also made my present plight all the more difficult to take. Baby Morgan was absolutely stunning. I felt grumpy and first, but her smile melted my stubbiness. There is something about a baby's cute smile and giggle that puts most things into perspective. Not long after that, my youngest sister gave birth to baby Samuel. Again the pride and delight on my parents' face tore me apart. I wanted to make them proud and I wanted to make myself proud. It's an elusive wish.

My landlord wasn't impressed with the delay in my rent, because over the next few months I didn't pay anything. I was living on incapacity allowance and that, for me, is only £55 pounds a week. I couldn't live and pay my rent at the same time. I was hoping that the council would pay most of my rent. It took several months of waiting before I got a decision from the council. Ironically, through this period, I was writing more and more about my problems with depression. Darin had agreed that he would edit my chapters as I sent them, via email, to his address. I found that the experience of writing about my life and my varied ups and downs was, as Darin had suggested, quite cathartic and therapeutic. I remembered days when I was undeniably happy, the kind of really annoying happiness you see in films and cartoons. Those memories also hurt. I realized how much I had lost and how much I have changed. During this period, I received some phone calls from Darin, my agent. At first, perhaps because I'm cynical and I hate the world I live in, I wasn't really sure how much of my work Darin had actually read. I felt incredibly honoured and privileged when he talked to me over the phone about work that I had written. He made he made me see that my dream of becoming published was more attainable than I have ever believed. It was with sickening amount of pride that I told my parents and anybody else that would listen, including our cat, that my agent had spoken to me on the phone for over thirty minutes about my possible novel. Though in this period I was feeling as low as ever, my work volume actually increased. I won't lie and say that I truly believe my work was good enough to be published, but it was a lovely, galvanising feeling that just maybe, if I was very lucky, it could happen.

When I was living at the house in St Annes in Nottingham, I got on well with a guy called Michael. He was a few years younger than my dad, but I really enjoyed his company. On days where I wrote about my life, I felt much better about myself. It was constructive to write and it took my mind off my latest cause for panic, paying the rent. Ironically, though I was writing about my past, which included some worse times than I was in presently, I always ended up feeling slightly better about myself. There were many days where I didn't write. I would just stay in bed or stare out of the window for hours. Just wasting time because I couldn't see the point in leaving my room or doing anything more constructive.

During this period, when I learned that my elder sister was coming home for a visit, I tried to rouse myself and get back into training. If I lost some weight and felt more comfortable about myself, I might be more at ease when I went home to see my sister, who stayed at my parents. I'd run for maybe, two or three consecutive nights. Up the hills, without stopping. I even returned to the gym for a week. But, I just saw myself as a failure and no amount of training was going to change that. I wanted to fight and bear my teeth. Show that I sick and tired of feeling downtrodden. I couldn't make a start. It was the same questions the caused me all the damage. Did I really believe in myself? I had lost the enjoyment of running. It made me feel better about myself and offered me a little hope. I wish I could just enjoy running for what it is and not use it to propel myself to try and lose weight in a ridiculously short space of time. If I did not feel like I was looking good enough, I wouldn't go out. I put pressure on myself because I constantly hated the way I looked in the mirror. My dad would ask me to go out for the night and have a drink with them. Part of me was desperate to go. I wanted to let my hair down and relax. Yet, the controlling and doubting part of my nature dominated. I looked in the mirror and saw a fat, bearded stranger staring back. Well, not even staring. I couldn't look at myself in those eyes. I refer to myself as a 'stranger' because I didn't know who I was anymore. Everything seemed to come down to failing at university. What did I have if I didn't have that dream? I had the dream of becoming published but to believe in something means that you have to be able pick yourself up if all went wrong. I didn't really believe that anything I could write would be of any interest to anybody else, even though Darin was constantly encouraging me. It got to a stage where I was far safer not to believe.

Days where I did actually venture out of my room, I would sometimes end up in Mick's room and I'd feel more relaxed for a while at least. I spent a few drunken hours with Mick. He was also suffering from depression and having a stroke as well which worsened his condition. We had quite a lot in common and at least for a few hours, I had a friend who I could talk to about my battle against the world. One time when my sister came to visit with Lee, I met them in Nottingham city centre. For some reason I enjoyed myself. Again, I have to refer to the way I looked. Scruffy bloke with a beard. I know I keep refereeing to my image but it pretty much spoke volumes for how I was feeling inside: unkempt. However, on this occasion, I allowed myself to forget who I was and relax.

I was about to take a huge risk. In my hands was a clear, plastic folder and in the folder were chapters 6 to 8 of this book. It was a huge gamble because I had never allowed any of my family to read the contents. Of course, the book is about my life, but it also touches upon my family's life as well. I hugged my sister & Lee goodbye and left feeling happier that I had dared to take this chance. I was a little on edge because I was afraid of my sister's reaction to my book.

I got a text later that evening from my sister. She told me she loved what I had written and that it gave her a clearer picture of what I had been going through all the years of my life. She wanted the rest of it. I thought carefully about whether or not to send her the rest of the chapters. My sister and my dad are really close. In the early chapters I make some strong critical comments about the way my dad treated me. Was I prepared to risk my relationship with my sister? I sent her over fifty pages all told. She read the work in a day and text me and wrote to me to say yes, my father would be hurt by the content but he would also be very proud. My 'dark' days with my dad are well in the past.

For a while, my sister's reaction to my work had made me feel a little stronger. Not long after her text, I received a letter from the council informing me that the council were prepared to pay £40 of my £65 a week rent. Because I hadn't paid anything for a few months there was also a shortfall of around £400 that I owed my landlord. My landlord phoned up the day after the letter from the council and told me I would have to find the £400 fast. I panicked. I couldn't give him what I didn't have.

A few days I had my first session with the Clinical Psychologist. She told me she believed that she could help me, but it would mean being patient. I told her of the mess I was in financially and she put me in touch with a council advisor. I was advised to leave where I was living and go home. My parents offered to let me live back home for a while. I was relieved at having that option. I still have to pay the landlord, but not until I'm earning again. That may be a while.

So I was going to return home again. At 31 years of age, soon to be 32 on January 16th in the new year, I felt honoured that I at least had the option of living at home. Again, I was going to have to face Christmas and New Years Eve and fight my way through my depressive thoughts. What worried me most was the strain I put on my parents. My mother is suffering with her basic mobility because of a problem with her spine. Before I moved to university and twice while I was living in St Annes, I was taken into hospital because I had fallen into diabetic comas. I have always been lucky that no long-term harm has befallen me. My dad is always the one who has to come and fetch me from the hospital and on the last occasion he had to come and bring me back home, which was at around 4 o'clock in the morning. He told me then that I was putting too much strain on him and my mother. He was right and, to be fair to myself, I haven't had any problems since then.

I didn't want to have to move back home and have my parents worry about my health when they had their own problems to worry about. The thought of having to go home again might well inspire me to become a better, stronger person. I was still producing work at a really impressive rate. I wanted to finish this book. Working with a proper 'shrink' was another reason to be optimistic. I hadn't spoke to one since I was a young boy. Surely that was going to help me. Nicola, the woman I'm seeing, told me she believed she could help me get to the point where I could help myself.

CHAPTER TWELVE
SUICIDAL THOUGHTS

I suppose depression and thoughts, and then, eventually, attempts at suicide, go hand in hand. What I would like to be able to accomplish is to reveal to you the incredible depths and sickening lows that eventually forced me to look at myself one last time in the mirror and ask myself, out loud, do I want to live anymore? Have I got the will to keep picking myself off the ground and then falling back down again? Do I care enough about the hurt that I'll cause through my suicide? What is there in death that will make my plight any more comfortable?

It's hard to recall specific times and dates. Not surprisingly, years ago, I didn't expect to be writing a novel on my battle with life! I wish I kept a dairy, but then again, I've always thought that only girls keep them. Way back in the mists of time when I was struggling to decide what college to go to and struggling even more to get a real grip on my life, I remember I was in our garage, which is situated at the side of our house. I write 'garage' but I should really be more specific. My dad had built one garage and two sheds. In fact, he's recently knocked one shed down and rebuilt it again. My elder sister, when she was home, referred to this new shed as my dad's 'Wendy House'. All this building and renovating of sheds has taken place over the last twenty or so years. It makes me laugh, and often cheers me up because despite the time it takes my dad to knock these creations up, once they're all standing, he just throws all his tools into them without any thought whatsoever. Trying to find something in any shed, and to a lesser extent the garage is like looking for the lost sock in the wash…. impossible!

Anyway, I remember looking at myself in the long mirror in the garage. I was in there because I was training and sweating my way, through songs on an old tape recorder, to lose weight. My image in the mirror would spur me on to greater effort. I can't remember why I was training. I love to be fit and run and train, but there was always a specific reason. Either I was going out with some friends or there was a party or something. I remember staring at myself for a long time. When I was younger, and when I was feeling low or down at heart, I used to glare at my reflection. I would have of made a great guard dog. I hated, absolutely despised myself at times. I used to punch myself in the face as well. Ironically, I was safer when I felt this way. I still hated myself but at least I was showing some kind of spirit. There was a fighter there. I could see in the mirror. The more serious occasions occurred when I looked in the mirror and just pitied myself. There was still loathing and hate, but it was immersed in pity and sorrow.

On this occasion I think that looking in the mirror didn't spur me on. The desired effect was to inspire myself, but sometimes I saw the sorrow in my eyes and, perhaps, I saw the truth as well - no matter how hard I trained or how good I looked, I couldn't keep my vicious thoughts at bay. I mean thoughts of how bad I looked and how, even then, I didn't believe my life would actually amount to anything. I remember I had a razor with me. Don't panic, it was a crappy disposable one. I looked at myself in the mirror and started hacking at my wrists. God it hurt! I winced and cried. The tears were for the pain, but also for my state. I wanted to die in that garage. It was a bitterly cold night and I had taken a blanket in with me to keep warm. I remember feeling cold, not physically, but emotionally. I had enough, even at such a young age.

I may have been twenty, perhaps a little older. I can still see the marks on both my wrists. They are very faint, but they are there, and always will be. After I hacked away for a while, I realised that I wasn't able to get enough of the blade to penetrate my skin. By now, after I had continued cut away, wy wrists were a mess. They were sore but at least I was still alive! I did look for a 'Stanley Knife' amongst my dad's tools. These have long and sharp blades. I didn't find one. To be honest, by that time, I was not as keen on the idea of dying. Had I found one I don't think I would have used it. I suppose this was a 'cry for help', though to be honest, I'm not comfortable with that train of thought. I know what the essence of it is, but people like me have to be in a certain mind set to even consider harming themselves. There was, even if it was only for a brief, fleeting moment, a time in that garage when I wanted to die. I was lucky. People who use the 'cry for help' attitude are only one step away from death. You know what's frightening about that? How long does it take to reach the next step? How much pain did I have to endure to bring me to this step? I looked in the mirror and I saw a person with no hope in his eyes. That is a horrible, awful thing to have to encounter. If you feel you have no hope you can fight and cling on for a while. If you look into the mirror and see a person staring back at you who is lifeless and devoid of spirit, it's very unsettling.

I left the garage, ironically, feeling even worse about myself than before. I was walking to our back door moaning and 'slagging' myself off for not even being able to kill myself. I was still alive, I had the cuts on my wrists to prove it. My mum and dad were out for the night. My elder sister was sitting in the front room watching TV. I slumped down in the chair next to her. We didn't speak. I was feeling pretty low, but I wasn't going to tell my elder sister why. I had covered my wrists with a jumper I was wearing. My sister saw my wrists. This was not intentional. She was really shocked and upset. She asked me if I minded her phoning our diabetic nurse, Karen. I said no, it was fine. It must have been her home number. It was arranged that I would go and see Karen the next day.

I promised my sister that I would go, and I did. I felt numb and confused. I knew what I had attempted but it felt like it had happened to somebody else. The following day I had an appointment at around 4'clock. I walked all the way there, to the hospital, I mean. It's about five miles, I should have been proud of myself for that alone. Karen offered some kind of help. Ironically, I still didn't get to speak to a 'shrink'. I was grateful for any help that came my way. I walked home as well. All of my family, apart from my youngest sister, were waiting for me in the kitchen. That scared and stunned me. Why hadn't I told my parents how I was feeling? There is no answer to that question. If you tell someone that you are feeling so low and depressed that you are seriously considering ending your life, then I suppose you'd be expecting a reaction and wanting some kind of help. For me, I was past that stage. I write stage, I never told any of my family how bad things were. I wanted to die. No flourishing words or pretty adjectives here. It was my life and I had enough of it. Speaking to my family, anyone of them, would be like asking for help. I didn't want help, I just wanted to die. It was only for the smallest of moments, but it was there.

That was the first time I can recall that I wanted to die. There were other occasions when I felt pretty much the same, but I didn't have quite the same conviction. One time was just before my sister, my elder sister, phoned up and asked me to go to Jake's funeral. A few nights before that, I had taken a big overdose of insulin. I took the injection before I went to bed for the evening. Overdosing on insulin can cause a person to lose consciousness and if they're not treated quickly, the person can fall into a coma. This was a cruel thing for me to do because it would have caused my parents so much concern. I know that dying in the garage is not exactly a laugh either but with overdosing on insulin, I would have probably survived via the paramedic and my parents would be kept up worrying for hours. It's hard to be ethical and moral about different methods of killing yourself but you do think about those things.

As I've written previously, for me, Christmas and New Year were always the worse possible times to be around. I suppose this is the very essence of being alive. Giving to people you love and starting fresh should be the best of times. Though, while I was living at home, and most of the time this would mean that my elder sister was working away someplace, it would be my mum and dad and me and my youngest sister. To be around a family at Christmas time is really about sharing the excitement of the whole festival package. I'd buy presents for my family and wonder what I would receive as I looked under the tree. I would say ninety percent of my whole persona at this point was an act. My mum, and I love her dearly for it, put the decorations up on her own. She made a real effort to lift the 'Christmas spirit' in our household, especially when my little sister moved out. By now, I had perfected the pretence of normality. I made out that I was ok and I could handle everything. I would often cry myself to sleep with my hand covering my mouth because I didn't want my parents to know how I was really feeling. When suffering from depression, the Christmas period is evil. You have to pretend because if you let your real feelings become known, you'll ruin everybody else's Christmas.

On New Years Eve of 1994, I made another attempt at ending my life. I have already written about this in a previous chapter so I won't repeat it all over again. Want I want to do is share with you the horrible, bleak emotionless void that filled my heart. The thing about feeling so low that as hard as you dare look, you simply cannot see a tomorrow is that it does not happen over night. There is an accumulator ticking away and sadly for me, whenever I feel really low and I'm struggling, my own accumulator seems only to remind of sad or negative memories. When I was feeling really low on New Years Eve of 1994, I stood over the precipice and all I could see was dark and black. No light, no silver lining and no horizon in site. It had been building up for months, in truth years. I had spent so much time was telling myself that I could pull myself though, that I would come out the other side and be a success. I was lying to myself because, in truth, I never really believed what I told myself. I was 21 at the time and I had heard, throughout my life, that it was a great age to be alive. Many times I can recall my dad or my mum or others tell me how they wish they were 21 again.

I felt absolutely shattered and beaten. I didn't want to see my reflection on the mirror because I was so ashamed at myself. I felt I was wasting my life away because I was only 21 and yet life had been such a struggle. It always seemed that everybody was happier than me and that, of course they had problems, but they had problems they could share with friends. I was on my own again. No friends to call on and that makes a huge difference. Continually lying to yourself and lying to those around you takes a hell of a lot out of you. It's like when I was at Bodelwyddan. In the daytime, I was smiling and joking and I was utterly professional as I instructed sports sessions. When I was on my own and in my room, I broke down. Stifling my sobs because I didn't want anybody else to know what I was going through. The act of pretending day in and day out is so completely draining. I was a great actor. Yes, there were occasions when I would feel really down at work, but I'd hide my true feelings with anger. I'd get angry about my situation and in turn, take my anger out on others, usually staff who I could get away with being angry at.

I even put on my act at the New Years Eve of 1994. My parents went out at around eight o'clock and I wished them a good night. I was slightly drunk by that point. I didn't intend on trying to kill myself at that point. I wanted to get drunk so I wouldn't have to cry in the New Year. I wanted to dance and shout and sing like normal people. I knew it was very sad spending New Years Eve on my own and getting drunk. The alternative was to sit and watch the clock and grow even more upset and anguished at the thought of another year of exactly the same oblivion. Even before this night, I thought long and hard about death and suicide. It takes time to get to that point though. I had been fighting for a long time, and the thought kept festering inside me that I had nothing to live for. I might try to fight this downward spiral by getting a job or going out or by training harder, but I would always end up in the same, cold, stagnant position of self loathing and awful, probing questions that I knew I didn't have the answers to.

I'd lie on my bed and ask myself what harm my death would do my family? Did they deserve to suffer years of torment and anguish? No, that's not quite true. I did ask those questions, but some part of me always replied that my family wouldn't really miss me anyway. I was doing them a favour by throwing away my pitiful life. I'd imagine my funeral and who would be there. I'd cry more and eventually fall asleep. Before a person arrives to the moment where they have decided that they can longer fight on, they've already been fighting for a long time. The agony that I put myself through as I weighed up the pros and cons of living is an awful, heart bleeding experience. I would spend a lot of time, lost in thought, balancing out the extremes.

As I look back, I'm surprised that I didn't become angry or frustrated. Why should I have to live like this? Why should I keep it all in and not let others help me? I had gotten to a stage where I had become so isolated that I didn't believe that telling my family would help. I mean, how the hell could I tell my family? I couldn't sit next to any of them and bleed my heart out. To tell them that life was so difficult that I was on the point of suicide was just not an option. I couldn't grow angry or frustrated because I felt, at that time, so utterly lost and alone. I do think some part of me was screaming for attention and help. I do believe that I have, in the past, made attempts on my life that were designed to get the attention of my family and the authorities. I cannot recall all these events. They were quite some time ago. This time, I wanted to prove to myself that I was serious.

At the point, in 1994, I felt so very alone. It was New Years Eve and too late to cry my heart out. I wanted everybody to know that I was really depressed, that it wasn't an act that I put on to get some attention or because I was too lazy to work. If I told people how I was feeling, some part of me believed that it would just be assumed that I was feeling a little down and all I wanted to was to talk and get a little attention. If all went to plan, I would have died on the 24th of December 1994. Without a shadow of doubt, people would then be forced to believe that I really was as sad and depressed as I told them I was! But I would have been dead! It confuses me now. It would have been dead but at least I would have proved my point and reclaimed some authenticity and respect.

I was under a lot of pressure from all areas of my life. Most of the pressure was put on myself. Little things like walking to the shops or talking to neighbours I could define as pressure because I looked a mess and inside I felt a mess. I didn't want to have to look people in the eye and talk to them. There were pressures from having to go and see Social Security and explain why I wasn't fit enough to work. Sometimes my money would be delayed or I'd send in a 'sick note' late. I would have to go into Nottingham city centre and explain to the Social Security staff that I was depressed and my money was delayed. They were cold and blunt and never tried to hide that they were scornful of my 'apparent' health problems. They didn't believe I was ill and I couldn't prove it to them either. What hurt was the fact that I had come under suspicion. I was seen as another statistic that was raping the economy by claiming benefits that I did not deserve.

The problem with depression is the person suffering from it cannot see what it is that causes them so much misery. If you have a broken leg, you can show people the cast and all the amusing messages written on it. The doctor will tell approximately how long it will take to heal. You then know, roughly, that you will be back on your feet at some stage in the future. You can tell family or friends the same. With depression there is nothing you can point to. You have no idea how long, if ever, it will take to heal from this awful affliction. That's the worse part. You will never be able to go and get a progress report from the doctor. That's what I mean about the pressure of having to prove that you really are suffering and you are not cheating the country or anybody else. There is a hidden pressure of those of us who suffer from depression. As I stated earlier, I cannot prove I have depression. I have nothing physical to point to – it's just the way I feel inside.

Before coming to the agonising decision that I was going to end my life, I had gone through months, maybe even years of analysing myself and asking if I could go on with the fight. As I stated earlier, it's an accumulative effect, which takes place over years. I had cried enough tears for my family and I knew exactly the kind of effect my death would have. I think it was when I was living at home, before I got the job in Wales, I had been putting myself through the usual torment of wondering how long I could go on for. I remember a Saturday afternoon when I was walking around, in a daze of confusion, lost in morbid thought about the future. I decided I was desperate and I was heading for a collision with a possible suicide attempt. I walked into a shop and bought £30 worth of lottery tickets. This may not sound that desperate, but at the time, I did not have much money. I didn't win a penny!

At this stage, looking at my reflection in the mirror, I wasn't crying. I was absolutely devoid of emotion. I felt like a corpse, and must have looked pretty much like one as well. I was concentrating on exactly what I was about to do. I was about to take over 80 strong painkillers and, just to make sure, I was going to 'wash them down' with more alcohol. I was afraid, but I was even more determined to 'get the act over with.' It was just past twelve o'clock. Before I took the tablets I was thinking that either my parents would come home and that would brake my nerve or if I didn't hurry and take the damn things, I'd loose my bottle. I staggered to my room. I slumped on the bed and I remember staring at the blank screen of the television. I had threatened, albeit my threats were only to myself, to kill myself for years now. Did I really want to go through with it? I let the thought sift through my mind for a moment. I screamed out loud. I screamed and ripped open one of the packets and shoved about three or four tablets into my mouth. There is a horrible acrid, chalky taste with tablets so I leaned out and picked up my can of lager and without any more thought, I swallowed all the tablets down with the lager. I started to cry because I knew that I wasn't going to back down. Each time I swallowed more lager and tablets, I shuddered because the combination of the tastes and flavours was very unpleasant.

I scribbled a note. Remember my handwriting is the worst that you'll ever read..... if you can read it! The note simply read 'goodbye' and I wrote my name at the side of it. I lie on the bed and waited for something to happen. I had stopped crying by this point because I couldn't see the point any longer. It's something I hadn't considered. What went through my mind, and now as I look back, this is a real irony, I was afraid to close my eyes. I was scared that I'd never wake up again! So I lay on my bed and just wondered what I had done to myself? I must admit that the longer I lay there, the more I thought about calling for an ambulance. I remembered that I would never get to see my eldest sister again. Earlier in the night I had phoned my younger sister and told her I loved her. To be honest, this conversation saved my life because the party where my sister was, she decided to leave early because she was worried about me. I tried to phone my eldest sister but she, like all normal people, was busy having a good time. My parents had already returned and I stumbled down the stairs and hugged them and told them that I loved them. So I had already decided I was going go back to my bed, to fall asleep and never wake again.

My parents rumbled me. My youngest sister had rushed home and told them of her concern. They all came into my room and, of course, my mother discovered my pathetic note. Perhaps I should have been surprised that she could actually read my writing! The paramedics arrived early. I was asked what I had taken and when they discovered the empty tablet packets they changed the question to 'how many had I taken?' I was pretty annoyed that I had been roused. The paramedics wanted me to walk down the stairs and I couldn't even stand. I was dragged out of my room and carefully lowered down the stairs. My youngest sister had her friend staying over and as I was put onto the gurney I saw both my sister and her friend watching me. My younger sister was not impressed by what I had done. Don't forget, it was yet another New Years that I had ruined.

It's hard to described how I was feeling. I think angry and confused is probably the best way to describe it. I was angry that I had been awoken, but I couldn't show my anger because I couldn't stand. In fact, I was strapped to the bed. I caught cold looks from my sister and my dad was angry with me as well. My parents had come home from a really good night and found that, yet again, I had ruined the good spirit. As I stated before this was the third or fourth year in a row that I had successfully ruined or greatly affected the spirit and atmosphere in the house. Sick and tired of fighting and duelling with the world, only to fall on my face and then have to go through the long, arduous process of getting my 'head back together'. I preferred death so desperately.

I had fallen asleep. I had not gotten up and told my parents because, I'd had enough.

I don't know what I expected to see once I opened my eyes again, but it was certainly not an ugly, but very efficient paramedic!

I had my system cleaned out in hospital and as I lay in the hospital bed waiting to talk to somebody from the Psychiatry department, it slowly, and painfully started to dawn on me exactly what I had done and how much pain I had inflicted. I tried to shut that topic of thought out of my mind, but it wouldn't budge. My mother was deeply upset by what I had done. My relationship with my dad would take many months before it felt right. The night before, as I lay on my bed and pondered life and death, I honestly felt I was doing the right thing. My death was the right option because it seemed that I had caused nothing but problems, arguments and heartache. I felt very strong in my conviction. Death was the only answer because it seemed to me at the time that I had exhausted all other routes.

But this was not entirely true. I was never given the opportunity to talk to a 'shrink'. It didn't enter my mind that I may not be successful in committing suicide. I hadn't thought about the difficulties and repercussions that an unsuccessful suicide attempt might bring. As I lay in the hospital bed, I really began to worry. How could I face my mother or my father or my little sister? I had ruined their nights and I could only offer an apology in my defence. I still felt inside that I was doing them a favour, but I knew my conviction would be as rubbery as my legs that night before if I actually spoke those words aloud.

I went home, in a taxi, with my mum and dad. I had with me one of those hospital grey vomit containers because all the 'stuff' they had pumped through my body was making me feel ill. The taxi driver told my parents that if any vomit hit any part of his car, there would be a £30 fine! So we drove home in silence, a horrible, uneasy silence that was filled with unasked questions and too many answers. I held out until I got home, and then ran upstairs and was sick. After a while of pretending to be busy in my room, my dad brought me some sandwiches to my room. He told me that my mother was very tired because she hadn't slept all night. Later, my sister wasn't in the house and my mum was still asleep. I ventured downstairs and found my dad in the front room. He was angry and, of course, concerned. He asked me if I realised what damage I was causing my mother? My reply was unforgivable and it was one time in my life that I wish I could go back and stop what I said. I looked at my dad with cold, pitiless eyes and I told him that before I took the overdose, I didn't care what he would think of my death. My dad thanked me for saying that. His exact words were, 'thanks, kid'. I knew I had hurt him and I instantly hated myself for it.

All the time I spent wondering about death I never gave a second thought to having to face my family if I survived.

It was like tiptoeing on broken glass. I didn't want to have to face anybody in the house. I felt so ashamed that I knew I didn't have a case to argue. I know that, as I inferred earlier, I was sick and tired of life. In my own my mind, I was doing the right thing. But when it came to discussing my point of view with my parents, my case fell apart. How could I tell them that I had considered their feelings but I had still came to the decision that I hated my life and I wanted to quit. Someone who makes an attempt on their life will have thought long and hard about the pain they'd be inflicting before they actually commit themselves to the act. In fact, it was that very argument that prevented me from trying to kill myself earlier - what about all the pain and suffering my death would cause to my family?

I did my best to try and avoid the rest of my family, but obviously, I would be able to do this for only a short space of time. In fact, the same day, New Years Day of 1994, in the early evening, I sat in our front room and apologised to both my mother and my father. They asked me what my plans were and I told them that I didn't intend to see the 'shrink' who I had an appointment with. I cannot remember why. I think it may have been a councillor and not a proper 'shrink'. I was adamant that I would recover using my own methods. Why they believed a single word I said I'll never know. I didn't believe it and it was me who was saying it! Later in the same year I got the job in Bodelwyddan and my life changed forever.... well, for a while anyway. Another problem I had was the question of trust. Would any of my family ever trust me again? I have been suffering with depression for a long time now. The incident at New Years Eve of 1994 is a long time ago and I am still fighting and not living life. I don't know what my parents think about that time but I don't think they'll ever forget it either. It makes me wonder what goes through my parent's mind as we approach Christmas and New Years each year. Not surprisingly, it is not something that we tend to talk about much. I do regret what I did now. It is only something that I can think about because I survived. I hate to think about what would have happened if I didn't survive.

The pressure is obviously at its greatest when people like me, are so lost that death seems to be the only answer. To try and ease some of this pressure I would go for long runs, including as many hill as I possibly could. My fitness has never been an issue. Sometimes going for long runs would enable me to forget about my problems. Instead, I would concentrate on my breathing or the next hill I had to climb. By the end of the run, most of the time, I'd look at myself in the mirror and hate what was looking back at me. I'm angry now as I recount these times because I should have been damn proud of myself! I used to run long distances and my mind was dominated by negativity. 'What's the point? Why should I bother?' Despite being weighed down by these leaden thoughts I persevered. I used to go for long walks as well. Whilst walking I felt free and weightless. The problems were there but I was, for the time being, coping with them. When I knew the therapy of walking was over, my mind persisted in its ruthless assault. That's when my mind became frantic and desperate. Despite my best attempts, I was back in the same position.

At this moment in time, though things are not great, they're not as bad as they have been. I'm seeing a Clinical Psychologist twice a month. My psychologist tells me she can help me change the way I think about things. We'll see. I hope so. I do not know if this manuscript will be published. I hope it is. Of course I do. I will not lie and claim that I will never try and kill myself again. If things continue to improve, then I will make a real attempt to put one hundred percent into my life. The fear for me is that I do know, when times are truly unbearable, that I do have the capacity to take my own life. That is an unnerving thought because I absolutely know it is true.

The thought of death or suicide has never left me from that moment in 1994. For years I had threatened and eventually I nearly delivered. That bridge, the construction of going from threats to actual commitment has changed everything forever. Now if I think of death of killing myself I know it is not for affect. I used cry myself to sleep, listening to sad songs and imagining who would be at my funeral. Now I know I am capable of 'completing the job' my thoughts are focused on what I'll miss out on and, of course, the harm I will have caused. It's hard to explain. Before the incident took place on New Years Eve of 1994, it was like I viewed my own death and those at my funeral through the eyes of a Hollywood film director. Today, it's with more reality, with a biting, piercing reality that I now think about suicide. There is no glamour, only tears and sadness and regret.

CHAPTER THIRTEEN
TALKING TO SHRINKS

I do believe that a problem shared is a problem halved. However, the problems that I was having in my life, I chose to share with very few people. I needed to talk to somebody and I couldn't rely on my family. In fact, apart from an occasional heart-to-heart with my mother, and sometimes my sister, I don't even let my family inside my head to see all the shadows that lurk there. Once, when I'd just moved to my new address, after coming home from university, I went home to visit my mum. For the past year, she has been pretty ill. A problem has developed with vertebrae in her spine, connecting with nerves in her back. It means she has very poor mobility and any movement leaves her in severe pain, accompanied by howls of anguish. In the next few months, she's scheduled for an operation.

I went home and to be honest, I was feeling really down. Thoughts of suicide were frequent visitors in my mind. I had lost my job. I was still brooding over the mess at university and I was waiting for a decision on my Incapacity Benefit application. Life was like a Monday morning, filled with rain and endless grey skies and clouds. If there's no 'shrink' or counsellor to talk to, then, ninety percent of the time, I'd 'bottle' everything up until something has to crack. That's what happened on this occasion. I started out having a conversation with my mother and ended up flowing with tears in front of her. I hadn't cried for a long time. I felt pressure from all sides and angles. Worst, so much worse, was the dreadful feeling that I was being forced into staring down the barrel of the gun again, and I felt death was the only place I'd find peace.

Those who suffer with depression, in my experience, often feel comfortable talking about their problems only in the presence of somebody who is qualified to listen, and perhaps offer some constructive advice and answers. Even when I was happier and I was living in North Wales, I still had problems. They were not so bad because I had a girlfriend and some good friends. I did confide in my girlfriend and it was good to get the murky past out into the open. It lifted some of the pressure from my shoulders. I still need to talk and 'let off steam' but I need some kind of constructive response. I need to tell someone how bad I'm feeling, but at the same time, I hope to hear some words of advice. I am, at the moment, seeing a Clinical Psychologist. When I speak to her, because of all I've been through and my age, I hope that I can take away more positives from my sessions with her.

When I was younger, I had many problems with my parents and this was basically because of bed-wetting. My parents made an appointment to speak with a child Psychologist. It wasn't too bad because I missed an afternoon from school! But then again, it was junior school and I loved my time there. I was only a kid so I didn't know what to expect. I cannot remember if I expected this 'Psychologist' to wave a magic wand and make everything good in my world. Later in life, when I was about 22, I was accused of expecting just that! On this occasion, I was with my parents, and looking back, albeit a long way back, that was not a good idea. I felt very nervous and extremely uneasy about the concept of speaking to a complete stranger on a very private and personal matter. To make things worse, the private conversation I was expecting actually took place in front of my parents and another doctor. My unease continued and I slid further and further down the chair I was sitting in. To make matters worse, I'd be suddenly asked a question, and I'd have to answer it. I had all these 'grown ups' watching me expectantly as I mumbled some kind of reply. It was almost as if I wasn't even in the room.

My dad, at this time, was clearly not happy with him being in the room. There was a combination of sins that probably fed his frustration - he was angry and embarrassed his son needed therapy in the first place. The second reason was my dad had never really believed in specialists who treat the mind. It's not a criticism because, let's face it, there are millions of people who don't believe in the kind of therapy that Psychologists and Psychiatrists offer. He always held this belief and I respect his opinion. However, at this time in my life, my relationship with my dad was not very good. I remember he was sitting at the side of me and all I was thinking was that I hoped the session wouldn't take too much longer because my dad was getting really angry. When it came to talking about my bed-wetting problems and the possible reasons for this, I was squirming like a nervous eel. My dad had insisted that the reasons I bed wet was because I'd lay there and let it happen or because, and he said this out loud, that I masturbated. You can see why I was horrified when I realised my parents would be in the same room.

I can look back at this time and state with absolute certainty that the meeting was a waste of time. I was tense and nervous and I think both of my parents were uneasy about being there. Who could blame them? It isn't an ideal situation for one of your children to be talking to a 'shrink'.

Perhaps it made them feel that is was them who were being analysed, scrutinized and criticized rather than me. It would have been far more helpful to me if I was able to talk to the 'shrinks' on their own. I would have felt much better and more at ease talking about the problems. I don't remember there being a follow up appointment.

A few years later I saw another 'shrink'. Again my parents were both present, but this time the mood was much more gentle and seemed far less volatile. The upshot was that I fill in a bed-wetting chart and my dad would learn to live with my problem. I remember that when I saw the 'shrinks' for the first time, the room was huge and the seating was very formal - hard backed chairs. The approach of the second 'shrink,' as I recall, was more upbeat and affable. It was a woman we spoke to and her attitude was more relaxed and that put my parents and myself at ease. I don't remember the names of any of the doctors and the therapists I saw, either when I was younger, or later on in life.

Years later, before I worked in Wales, I was talking to a counsellor at my doctors surgery. I cannot remember all of the counsellors that I have spoken to, but it's far more than I like to admit. Before seeing this counsellor, I'd seen quite a few others before her. The deal is, you sit in a chair, usually opposite the person that you're talking to. The counsellor's chair is in close proximity to your own. The alternative is to have a large space dividing the counsellor and yourself. You tell the counsellor, or 'shrink,' what is on your mind, what it is that's bothering you. This can take some time because it's hard to 'open up' in front of a stranger, even if they are qualified to listen to you. If there's a large space between you and the counsellor, often you can see that as a barrier, as if they're not really listening, but more intent on judging you. When you're nearer to the person you're talking to, you feel more of a bonding, a togetherness that makes you feel that you are being listened to and understood. The lack of space between you and the counsellor is indicative of the ease at which you're able to trust in this person. I once saw a male counsellor and again, I remember the room being really quite large and there were two chairs in this room and they were miles apart. On this occasion, I was on my own. The gentleman I was supposed to confide in was dressed in a very smart and very formal suite. I remember he wore glasses and he had, perched on his knee, a clipboard that he wrote his notes on. That hit me as soon as I walked though the door. His image and his manner and the fact that we were supposed to hold a very serious and personal conversation ruined it for me. I took an instant dislike to the man and consequently I found I couldn't 'open up' and trust him. When you have to talk about pressing issues foremost on your mind, the anxiety that you experience in the days and hours, and sometimes weeks before you actually get to talk to somebody qualified to listen, and you have somebody that you do not feel you can speak to or bond with in any way is a huge, and I mean HUGE disappointment. It is really very stressful and extremely nerve-racking when you have tell a complete stranger your history and fears and fleeting aspirations. It does not help when, as you deliver the extremely difficult words, you've conscious of the large space in between the counsellor and yourself.

The counsellor I was referring to earlier, the one I saw at my doctor's surgery, was far more relaxed and, very importantly, she was much more informal. I mean what she wore and they way she spoke and way she treated me generally. That put me at ease straight away. The fact that as soon as I was in this woman's presence, I felt my body relax and mind relax. The session took place in what can only be described as a 'cosy' little room. I noticed that the two chairs in the room were close together and the room itself was casual. Pictures on the walls, cushions on the seats and plants and flowers in various places around the room. It was not clinical nor as cold, emotionless, as the rooms that I had been in before. It appeared to be a normal room for conversations to take place in. It had a comfortable, sedate atmosphere. I observed these things within seconds of seeing them, and it helped me relax.

There is no hiding from the fact that however nice the person is you're talking to, or whatever colour scheme the room is in, talking to a counsellor is a emotionally draining experience. If, on your first impression, you feel that the room in which these very important sessions take place is a room, rather than an office, then it's comforting and puts you in a more relaxed frame of mind, and the difficult part of actually talking and 'opening up' is easier. There was a stark difference in the look and feel of the room at the doctor's surgery and the rooms that my sessions took place in earlier. Even at such a young age I just 'knew' that the environment was all wrong. Far too cold and austere for anybody, let alone a small boy to open his heart in.

The hardest part, for me anyway, is getting started. I suppose there is certain irony in this 'getting started' process because I never actually know where to start. I've seen many different counsellors, and I think my start has been different on every occasion. It always terrifies me. At the start of the session, when I've first been introduced to the counsellor, I'm pretty reserved and non-committal. I listen to what they say, and inside, I know it'll be my turn to talk son and that's when the show of bravado and exterior that I live is peeled away. I live my life as a complete lie and falsehood. I pretend to find something funny because that's what 'normal' people do. In fact, I hate leaving my house. I'm much happier at home, reading my books and staying warm. But, that's not a life. I'm hiding away and by talking to a counsellor, I'm admitting that I need help. For the first few minutes, before I open my mouth, and while the counsellor is telling me what kind of session and how she may help me, I still feel that I'm the person who lives his life as a lie. When it is my turn to speak, that person living the lie, for as long as I'm in that room talking to a qualified listener, is silent. I know that if I'm not honest and open with this person, then there really is no hope for me.

Once I've decided where the hell I start, I'm like the 'Duracell' rabbit. You know, the one that goes on and on forever. It's a race to get as much as I can out in an hour. I start out tense and sitting up in my chair. I'm very nervous at the start of each new session and it shows in my posture and manner. What needs to be understood, right from the outset, is that I am opening up to such an extent, that I am trusting this stranger, I know it's a qualified stranger, but still, technically, the person sitting opposite me is a stranger. Yet, I am telling them things that I would never tell anybody else. Not even family or close friends or even when I had a girlfriend. I tell this outsider some deep and private things about myself, and there is never, or very rarely a flick of emotion or any sign that this person is in judgement of my life and me. I mean, what you are doing essentially is giving yourself over to the counsellor, placing complete trust in them and hoping that they can offer to you the right words and that much needed advice.

I know now that the first few sessions with the counsellor are designed for you 'get off your chest' all that is bothering you. Bearing in mind that a session is more often than not about an hour in length, it still isn't that much time to 'bleed out your heart'. In my experience, I want to go away from the session, whether it's the first one or not, with some constructive advice or a piece of information that I'll be able to use as a shield or as some kind of tool against all the problems that I've encountered in my life. I had that attitude when I saw this counsellor at the doctor's surgery. I was told, in polite but direct terms, that I should not go into these sessions and expect the counsellor to wave

a magic wand and make everything better instantly. She
told me that I had my part to play as well. I agreed, but I
still hope to leave the session feeling empowered and I still
hope to have learned something that can help me fight this
losing battle.

After a few sessions with this counsellor, I felt more
trustful of her. It takes time to feel completely at ease and
have total trust in somebody. She was concerned about
the way I viewed myself. Specifically the problems I had
with my weight and the way gaining weight made me feel.
At one point, she told me she wanted to refer me to see a
Clinical Psychologist. I had, and to be honest I still have no
idea what a Clinical Psychologist actually does. It sounded
good to me because it sounded like progress. More help
to put 'humpty' back together again. After a few more
sessions seeing this woman, she suddenly told me that, in
her opinion, we had come to the end of our time together.
There was nothing more she could do for me. It came as
shock. I didn't ask about the Clinical Psychologist. I was
hoping that I would hear something in the post within the
next few weeks. I had no more correspondence whatsoever.
I didn't ask her there and then, because I didn't want to hear
that there was no meeting or appointment made for me. I
would rather have a glimmer of hope than nothing at all.
I wish I hadn't though. If I had simply asked her, at least
I wouldn't have spent weeks wondering and watching and
feeling what slim hope slip away.

The Clinical Psychologist I am seeing now, Nicola,
asked me if there is anything that I felt didn't work with the
methods used by the counsellors that I had seen in the past.
She was obviously told that I was the worlds leading expert
on counsellors. I sat back in my soft chair and thought
about the counsellor at the doctor's surgery. At first, like all
good counsellors, she made me feel at ease in her company.
After a while though, I couldn't help thinking that she

was treating me like an exercise in a textbook. It's hard to explain. Her answers were smooth and rapid in reply. I couldn't help but get the impression she had seen hundreds of cases like me and I was just another statistic to her. It felt like whenever I asked a question, her answers were so quick that they were not her opinions, but ones she read out of a book. I felt like I wasn't getting all her attention. To be honest, though I was shocked that our sessions came to such an abrupt end, I really wasn't too bothered about not seeing her again.

A problem I have found when speaking to counsellors, good or bad, is that many times when I'm out walking, I get this nagging question – at what point did all those people who killed themselves, through suicide, think to themselves that 'enough is enough?' In my experience, the very fact that I'm there and I've made the effort to be sitting opposite a counsellor is testimony to the fact that I want to fight on. I want to be helped and I'm prepared to do whatever it takes. I've ask myself 'how many more times can I do this?' Seeing a counsellor is obviously very important to me and those who suffer with mental health issues. It is a clear statement of intent. My concern is, when is it enough? A morbid thought, I know, but it does bother me, especially now. Whilst waiting to talk to a counsellor, I've often told myself that all will be well when I get to speak to them. Even now, after all the many counsellors I've seen, it is very hard not to see them and hope that they are the first step to salvation. That they will make enough difference in my life and guide me on some kind of course. My point about when is it 'the final straw?' comes about because, you have to put so much trust into a counsellor that as you sit there in their company, listening and talking, you have to feel that the reason you're there is because you're going to improve. What if you get a thought or a feeling that tells you dragging up the past and 'bleeding' out your heart to yet another stranger is not going to help you anymore?

When I was studying in Southampton, I saw the counsellor, Claire, before the real trouble had started. I must have become so used to falling into the same traps that I 'knew' I was heading for another fall. When I spoke to Claire, in a really small room, the chairs were comfortable and in close proximity. The main lights were off and the lighting came from a large lamp, placed in the corner of the room. I can best describe the lighting as 'subdued'. It was soft, not like some conventional lampshades.

I have always been able to make eye contact with whomever I was talking to, apart from one counsellor who actually came to our house to meet my parents. I had seen her in her office, but for some reason, she wanted to meet my parents as well. I cannot remember her name. She was good and I felt at ease in her company, well, up to a point. One of her eyes, her pupils, was permanently fixed in the same position. As I remember, this eye was always looking towards the right side of her skull. When I spoke to her, I was very conscious about her right eye. As I was speaking to her, at the same time I was telling myself to look at the bridge of her nose instead. Then, I told myself that she might feel hurt or offended if my vision was affected because I was now looking at her nose and not into her eyes. Instead of listening to her and absorbing her words and gaining comfort by them, I was trying to ignore her right eye. The reason that I mention this is because there has to be a unity between the counsellor and you. When you start talking, you become isolated. Cut off and set adrift. The hour you spend with a 'shrink' or counsellor is lost in an environment of silence and soothing. No distractions from outside.

When I saw Claire at Southampton she thanked me for seeing her before things were really at a bad stage. I was very nervous about seeing her. This was because it wasn't in the script. What did I need to speak to a counsellor for? I was at university wasn't I? This was where I was supposed to be in my element, having fun and making friends. Still, I couldn't have asked for a better person to talk to. By the time I was sitting opposite her, I had already decided that the end was nigh and I was absolutely destined to fail. It was Claire who pointed out to me that catastrophe was something that many people suffering from mental illness had in common. We all think, not only the very worse case scenarios, but also we think these devastations on a large scale. It was so much worse for me because I desperately didn't want to fail, not at university, which was unthinkable. Claire had a soft voice and she always seemed attentive. It helps, especially when speaking to a counsellor, if the listener appears at least to be interested in what you're saying. That way their replies and advice feels more authentic. I have walked away from sessions with counsellors, especially the one at my doctor's surgery, feeling that I wasn't really being given the attention I needed. I didn't really believe what I was told because the person wasn't paying attention to me.

The longer I saw Claire, which was about seven sessions in total, the better I felt in her company. I would tell her how I had so many damning and negative thoughts. They were suffocating me. They were affecting my work and my performance at university. When I was in her room and sitting opposite her, I felt incredibly relaxed. It was like working a twelve-hour shift and going home and lying on a bed of feathers. She made me feel completely at ease with myself and most importantly; while I was with her, I sensed a flicker of hope for the future. Problems started to occur when I was not in her company. Many times, as I walked home from my session with her, I'd look out onto the common and my mind would drift into familiar choppy waters. I later described this sensation to Claire. I told her that I felt like my mind was filling in the silences, the occasions when you have nothing to think about and your mind simply wonders and stumbles through all the clutter in your head.

When this happened to me, not just after the sessions but at any time, my thoughts turned back to negatives and questions. Did I really think talking to a counsellor was going to change anything? Did I really see any kind of future? I suppose the irony is that they are only questions. What harm could simple questions do? Yet, they were questions that I feared the answers to. I feared the answers because I always felt I already knew the answers to them. It was frustrating and frightening. On one hand I was proud of myself because I had sought the help and advice of a counsellor, somebody who could help me; and on the other hand I only felt that I could manage when I was in her company. I knew this was not a good sign. I have already written about the Halloween party we had in our halls. Everybody was so happy because we had just handed in our first big assignments. The party took place in the blue kitchen on Friday night. I had seen Claire earlier that day. Still, I couldn't cope. This was a very bad sign. I desperately wanted to enjoy myself to prove that I could see Claire and I could also have fun and relax in my spare time. The amount of effort I put into 'pretending' to enjoy myself made the fall even more prominent. I could see I was losing control again. It was even worse because I was talking to a counsellor at the same time. I should have been feeling stronger. It was a very bad night for me, and further confirmation that I was slipping deeper into depression.

From that moment on, life got worse and worse. My sessions with Claire were built up to such absolute importance that even before I talked to her, I was telling myself that I desperately needed her to make me feel positive. I was under so much pressure that I was expecting Claire to wave the proverbial wand and make things all right again. I did feel much better in her company, but even then, I was my own worst enemy. In our last few sessions, I spent time telling myself that I better remember what she said because it may be a week until I got to see her again. I knew soon after my session with her that I would start to ask myself those impossible questions and once that started, I was on the slippery slope again. At any time in a lecture or seminar, I would be trying to concentrate and at the same time my mind would be echoing with the same awful questions. I would fight and battle with this for hours each day. It made feel exhausted and it broke my heart to have to feel this way. I was witnessing my dream crumbling before my eyes. I could see what was happening and I felt so utterly powerless to stop it. It was pressure on top of pressure. I wanted to hide and lock myself away in my room. By this time, I had a conversation with my course leader who told me that I was okay if I missed a few lectures. It wasn't. I knew that if I missed one, I would cascade into a worse position, an impossible one.

Around this time I was supposed to be going home as well. More pressure. Each time I saw Claire I felt ready to cry. I was in a really bad way. Our appointments became more and more important. I was desperate to feel that something was going right. I needed to feel that I was back in control and I was making the right decisions. Seeing a counsellor was the right thing to do. I knew this. It made me feel as if I was on the right track again, if only for an hour. Claire was becoming concerned by my behaviour. She asked me what I would do if, hypothetically, one of our sessions had to be cancelled. How would I react to that? Those simple questions shocked me. She was right. I was depending on her far too much. Of course, some part of me already knew this. If, and it never happened, she did cancel a session, it would be a disaster for me. If I were thinking properly, I would simply make another appointment with her. I was floundering by this time.

I know I keep writing about 'pressure' and on the face of it, my pressures weren't so bad if I compare them to a heavy workload or a mother bringing up hungry children. But I was not thinking straight at this time. I was panicking. I didn't want to go home, but I had already bought a ticket and told my parents I would be home. I was finding it harder each day to turn up for lectures. I continued training, but I got no pleasure from it. I hated myself in the mirror. It wasn't long after that I told my parents that I wasn't coming home for Christmas and that Claire said she wouldn't be able to see me for three weeks. I can't and won't try and explain how I felt when I heard this news. Claire hugged my goodbye and told me that she expected to see me in the New Year. I didn't think that was very likely to happen. I knew I wasn't going to be able to cope without speaking to her for three weeks. She didn't leave me high and dry. She gave me a number to call if I was feeling really low and I needed to talk to somebody. It wasn't the same. I had built a special bond with Claire. I didn't want to have to talk to a complete stranger. I ended up talking to my local doctor and she put me in touch with a mental wing of a nearby hospital.

I don't blame Claire. She went off to visit her family; after all, it was Christmas. I realise that I depended on her far too much and I paid the price. I do believe that if my course at university had started earlier in the summer, say June or July, I would have stayed and possibly been able to complete to first year. I have learned that a counsellor will help you in the session. Talk and listen. I am now having sessions with a Clinical Psychologist. The sessions differ in the fact there is more interaction between talker and listener. More advice is offered in giving practical methods of how to deal with those difficult times when you're not sitting opposite the counsellor or Psychologist.

Today, as I write these words, I am living with my parent again. I still feel awful and my future is still very uncertain. I've been seeing another "shrink" for the past three weeks and this is a new experience for me. Firstly, Nicola is not a counsellor, but a Clinical Psychologist. This basically means there is more interaction. I get to see some kind of plan on how we, working together, will approach my problems. It isn't just about me talking for an hour and then having the counsellor explain, soothe and reassure me. At this stage, I think I need more than that to pull me out of the rut I'm in. I know from experience that I need more than just to have somebody listen for an hour. I need to be able to apply some kind of planned defence when I start asking 'those' questions. I have told Nicola my biggest fear is the time that I'm not speaking to her or when I relate my experience to university or further beyond that. She's told me that our sessions will be dedicated to simple methods employed to tackle negative thinking.

I must say I'm hopeful. From the first session, Nicola's approach has been different from counsellors that I've seen. For a start, and I found this really refreshing, she asked me what I thought were good and bad techniques from the people I had seen in the past. As a patient, that gives me hope straight away. It means that the person I am talking to is trying to impress upon me that she wants to help and welcomes feedback from me. I want to be taken seriously because this us a very important subject: it's my life! At the time of talking to her I was under a lot of stress. Not just with the way I was feeling, but also because my landlord had threatened to evict me. I wrote letters explaining what I was going through and why it was I wasn't working. I was waiting to see if the council would pay most of my rent.

So, I hope you will get some kind of insight into how I was feeling when I met her.

Also, Christmas is coming up and I can only relate everything to last year when I was at university. So I was under a lot of pressure. My meeting with Nicola went well. She relaxed me straight away and I've seen her twice since. As I stated earlier, my time with Nicola is more of team effort. She told me that sometimes it might be 3 weeks before I get to see her again. During the time, she wants me to be working on techniques to change the way I think. We haven't discussed anything but I remember a technique I was told about when I was on a 'confidence boosting' course. A little irony here because it was held in a college in Nottingham and a security guard showed me the room it was being held in. As we walked into the room we chatted and he told me he was surprised that I would want to do the course, as he thought I was confident.

The technique was called 'Thoughts-Feelings-Behaviour'. If I can remember rightly, the idea is to exchange a negative thought for a positive thought and subsequently that should influence your feelings and behaviour. The example used was the course tutor had to drive though the streets of Nottingham and because of her low confidence and self esteem, she kept putting it off. The problem became worse the longer she put it off. She then changed her thoughts from 'I can't drive because I'm scared I'll get lost' to something along the lines of 'I will drive and if I do get lost I'll ask for directions'. She drove and as she did so she began to feel more confident and behave positively. Me, being the perennial cynic, thought she had made it all up. I tried to apply it to my life but since I didn't believe it in the first place, I never stood a chance!

My sessions with Nicola have only been for a few weeks but they are starting to improve my confidence. I've had a shave in the last week. I started to go running (actually walking) again at night. This help me lose some weight and improve my health and diabetic control, and also I enjoy being out in the open air. It helps me think clearer. Nicola made a chronological linear map of my life and experiences.

I've never had this done before. Again it leads to believe that this person it listening and taking an interest in my life and my problems. We discuss how best to tackle these problems. This gives me real hope.

I still feel that I'm placing my life in another person's hands. I realise, of course, that I have so much to tell her and lots of input. Still there is no escaping the fact that I can only improve with the help of a trained specialist. I've lost count how many times that I have told counsellors and other specialist my life story. At the end, I walk home feeling numb. It isn't nice telling people what your fears and failures are. I suppose in an ideal world I would keep those things locked up and hidden away - just like the rest of the world. I'm very grateful to receive this and any other help that comes my way. I hope it works this time.

CHAPTER FOURTEEN
HOPES, DREAMS AND
ASPIRATIONS

Very rarely will you hear somebody suffering with a mental illness talk about hopes for the future. I have, pretty much, always viewed hopes and dreams from a distance and with more than a hint of envy. I suppose my dream, the one that carried me for so many years, was to be able to go to university and get a degree. Well, at least I went to university! I suppose there are 'ambitions' and there are 'dreams'. I can remember when I was a kid, on Sundays, my elder sister and I had to clean our bikes. It was a real drag because, as kids, we wanted to be screaming and teasing and running about. But my dad wanted us to clean our bikes. We used wire wool to clean all the chrome parts and because we'd still be fighting or teasing each other - to be more precise my sister teased me - it used to take us a long time. To make things worse, my dad used to play Abba albums on the record player while we cleaned our bikes, or worse still, he would play a Nolan Sisters' album. When I was in infants' school, my class had to write a letter to the TV show ' Jim'll Fix It'. It was about him making your dreams come true. In my letter, I asked to sing with Abba. As I grew older I cannot really remember having any dreams or ambitions. University and then college just seemed like the next logical step. Mind you, I would have liked to sign for Liverpool F.C.

As I reached my latter teens, life was horrible and all I wanted to do was hide away, which seemed the easy option. Dreams and aspirations are surely founded on mental strength and faith in, not just yourself, but also the future. You have to be able to live the dream. You have to believe that you can be part of it, you have to be living. Over the last five years, I have simply not dared to dream. Hanging onto life and surviving have been pretty much a full time occupation. When you're depressed, it's difficult to think about your ambitions when life is so bad that it's a real battle just to get through the day. In fact, I'm afraid to have dreams, as dreams can damage someone suffering from depression.

To believe in something, to put faith in something, means picking yourself up from the floor yet again and starting the very long road to some kind of redemption. What makes believing and daring to dream so fearful is the thought that after all the hard work I put into picking myself up, being able to face myself in the mirror, is knowing that I'm bound to fail again. History tells me that I'm on course to fall again and that is so dispiriting to me. The fact that I can write about 'my future' is some indication that part of me does feel there is a reason to live. Still, it's like walking a tightrope, the sheer gradient of belief and the very long fall back time and time again. Why dare to dream when you're just setting yourself up for failure?

I have always strived for my parents to be proud of me. I knew from a young age that I was a disappointment to them. Their only son didn't stop bed-wetting until he was 14 years of age. I think this issue has been smouldering for years. I felt much better about myself when I had a girlfriend and when I worked in Wales. I felt that was just the beginning, and I was on my way. Leaving and retuning home in February 2000 was a disaster. I cannot honestly remember the last time I truly felt proud of myself. It was probably when I went to my friend, Ian's engagement party, before my course at university started.

Perhaps what I'd like most of all is the easiest to actually achieve. I'm sick of being on my own. I don't mean having a woman on my arm so I can show her off like an accessory. I've never been that way. I just want everyone to know that I'm normal, that I can live a normal life and I can have a successful relationship. Over the past few years especially, I've seen my sister's boyfriends come and go. I always feel like the odd one out and it's a feeling that I hate. Last year, before I moved away into my own place, my elder sister was living at the house because she was waiting for her baby, Morgan Rhianna, to be born. Lee, her boyfriend, was also staying at this time. My youngest sister and her boyfriend came to visit. Obviously, the house was creaking under the strain of having so many people trample though it. There was quite a lot of excitement and anticipation in the air because there were two expectant mothers in the house - my two sisters. My older sister kept trying to wind my little sister up by telling her she looked really fat considering she was only in the early stages of labour. My younger sister is actually tall and very pretty. We all knew she was a little self-conscious about her figure during pregnancy. So the atmosphere in our house was very upbeat and lively. I felt I was the odd one out, again. I was the only person in the house that didn't have a partner. I felt alone and isolated.

It would make me proud to take a girl home and laugh at my childhood photos. I've been there and, though at the time I didn't think it was a particularly poignant moment in my life, now I would cherish the moment. I'd look forward to going back to Wales much more if I had somebody I loved sitting beside me on the journey there. I could relive my old memories with pride and give momentous events in my life the respect they deserve. I have a lot of happy and funny stories to tell, but nobody to tell them to. This isn't about a sad person who is too shy or complaining that life is too tough. I want a chance, another one, to make a go of my life.

I have only met my elder sister's daughter and I love her so very much. I felt drained when I heard my sisters were both pregnant because I realised how proud my mother and father would be. I first heard the news while I was in Southampton and my first reaction was that I was under even more pressure now to succeed and really make a go of it at university. I know it must appear warped that I didn't declare my love and happiness to both my sisters. I phoned them up and I told them how happy I was. Not entirely a lie because I was pleased for both of them - especially my elder sister because she had lost Jake Everton Baines a few years earlier. It wasn't just that both of my sisters were going to have children that caused me to much question myself. It was the whole issue of a family unit. When I had a girlfriend, the thought of marriage and children was not a 'hot potato' to me like it was to a lot of my friends at that time. At one point, I thought my girlfriend was going to tell me she was pregnant. It would have meant that we would have to have left Wales and lived with her folks or mine. I remember I was scared and concerned, but I wasn't objecting to the idea. Seeing the happiness that a my sister's baby has brought her, my present situation feels all the more severe and leaves me feeling even more stranded and along. A hell of a lot has to change before I can even dare spend a few seconds thinking about families and marriage. It's my greatest dream.

Being a dad, for me, would make this entire struggle seem worthwhile. I know I need to have a girlfriend to get this dream started, but this chapter is about my dreams and aspirations. Many people in life have been through a lot worse than me and still come out the other end smiling. Of course there's hope for me yet. My experience with my dad, in my early years, has taught me the lessons that he didn't have the time to learn. He was always working when I was young. I mean he worked from the darkness in the early hours of the morning until the darkness of the early evening. He and my mother had three children to bring up and there was no choice in the matter. My relationship with my dad is much better now, but it's been a long time getting there. Both my mum and my dad have done so well to bring three kids into the world. Of course, they're grandparents now and they love it! I know from my dad's mistakes that discipline and punishment can go too far. I believe that discipline is required at times. I also know from first-hand experience that too much discipline is not a good thing. If I'm lucky enough to find somebody I love and have children, especially a son, I'm sure I'd be a good father.

I've always wanted to be part of a group. What better group than my own family? I see the way my sister, my elder sister, is with her baby. I thought that I would only pretend to like Morgan, but I actually do lover her. I can see the enormous pride that my sister has in her family. What I wouldn't give for that feeling. I would love the idea of being responsible for a wife and children. The sacrifices my parents made for me are overwhelming. There's so much hard work involved in bringing up a family. I have a feeling within me that if I can survive these rough, desolate times, that I'll be a good parent. If I live through this, and I think that I will, I'll make a successful life for myself. I'll have the strength to survive anything. It's not much comfort now, because I still see a hard uphill struggle ahead. I have a long way to go before I can start dreaming of the future. But I hope I can look back on this stage of my life with pride because it took so much strength and tenacity to get through these days.

Before I can cast my net over such lofty ambitions, I really need to have some kind of perspective. One part of my life that has always upset and frustrated me is the burden and anxiety that I constantly cause my parents. Life would much better for all of us if I could live in my own place, but I tried that and ran into problems with my landlord. I'm at home again and what concerns me is that my parents have to see me on a daily basis. I wish, in an ideal world that I could have my little crisis and then go and see my parents. I am living this horrible existence right in front of their eyes and it cannot be easy for either of them, having such a disparity in the welfare and the happiness of their children. Their two daughters are both happy. It warms their hearts to see how happy and how well their daughters are doing. As for me.... it must be very difficult for them to see me struggle, time and time again. They have seen it throughout their lives and I'm sick of having to play the part. I would love to feel that when I spoke to my parents, they saw a confident and happy person, a person who is able to deal with the peaks and the troughs of life. I suppose it all comes back to my being able to feel that what I have to say is valid. My parents have never indicated that what I do or say is not important. The problem lies within me. But it is a problem that is affecting the way I behave and, although it is a rare occurrence, the way I interact with them. That is my fear. I feel so crap about myself that I feel that nobody wants to listen to what I have to say.

My dream is to feel comfortable with my family again, especially my parents. I always feel I have to make an excuse and hide away. I feel like the 'elephant man' sometimes. I crave the solitude of my small room because it means that I don't have stand in front of my parents and feel ashamed of myself. I don't want to have to think before I speak to them. I want get myself out of this rut and feel that I'm a valued part of a wonderful, loving family. The irony is I am part of this family and yet I feel at distance from them. I feel I'm watching my family grow older and live their lives, while I stagnate and hover between extreme lows and sickening confusion.

This dream can be tantalisingly close to reach. If I can start to have faith and believe in myself, then I can bridge this gap. It is down to me to make things right because my parents don't know how I feel. How do I go about explaining how I feel on this very delicate subject? My parents are really supportive of me and I wish I had the courage to explain why I am so quiet and so apparently out of touch with them. If I could feel that my parents no longer worried about me as much as they do, it would make me feel like their son again.

Another hope of mine is that I can have more of an influence over my weight. It is something that I have struggled with for years. I don't mean the weight problem. I'm about 5 feet 8 inches tall. When all is well and I have a more balanced approach to life, my weight is around 11 and half to 12 stone. When, like now, I start to struggle though life, my weight increases to over 13 stone. I'm not and have never been obese. I put on the weight because I know that I'll not be spending too much time out in public. I suppose it's comfort eating. I don't have any real friends and I rarely ever go out. Curiously, I don't derive much pleasure from eating chocolate and cakes etc. I do it because it has become part of me. It is a pattern that I always seem to follow. Even more bizarrely, it is the only regular pattern that I follow. Once I can see some kind of future outlined, like before I went to university or before I went to Ian's party, I will suddenly stop, and I mean completely stop, eating fattening foods to the point that I almost make myself ill. I'll train so hard and with so much determination that if I sat and pondered why the hell I couldn't put this amount of sprit into the rest of my life, I'd probably become depressed again!

I would love to just relax and feel that even if I did put a few pounds, or even a few stones, that it isn't the end of the world. So what! Everybody puts on weight. Weight fluctuates like the stock market. I'm tired of stuffing myself with food that I don't really like just because I'm on another 'snake' and not a ladder. Problems with my weight also have a bad effect on my already very fragile diabetic control. Eating too many sugary foods means my blood sugars are too high. If I go through a month of 'unhealthy' eating, I run the risk of my blood sugar being too high. If my blood sugar is too high, I will develop serious problems when I get older. I know all this and yet I still eat a very unhealthy diet at times. Similarly, when I start to train again, and by training I refer to 'running' or 'jogging', I train very hard. It makes me feel quite proud of myself that I can sprint up hills that most people struggle to walk up. I really enjoy this training, but sometimes, if I'm on course to loose a certain amount of weight in a certain amount of time, it gets past enjoyment and encroaches on to commitment. I have to run because I'm under pressure to look right at a certain time. The idea that if I don't run, I'll be in serious trouble because of my lack and control and discipline in my diabetic control, also forces me to run. The enjoyment soon dies off and I see it more as a rigorous test: no fun.

I would feel much more relaxed if I was more secure with my family and if I can find somebody to love me for just being me, I don't think the weight would be such a big issue. I like to be slim and I love knowing that I am very fit. It takes the edge off me when I run at night. It is a great time to think and see things in the proper perspective. The more I shut myself up and hide myself away, the more I view the world through negative spectacles. I know this, yet I find it very hard to do anything about it. That is why I hope I can continue to run and enjoy it for what it is. I feel like I can glide and run my worries and cares away. I feel no burden or stress or worry of any kind when I run. I want to be able to enjoy the exercise without attributing so much importance to it. It always ruins it for me in the end. The enjoyment dies out and I'm running, not because I enjoy it, but because I'm under pressure to loose weight far too quickly.

Because of the way my life has panned out, I do my best to avoid crowds. I've shut myself in and isolated myself from the rest of society. That probably seems a bit severe but it is true. When I was at university, England was playing Australia in the final of the Rugby World Cup. I had been following the tournament from the start, and watch a couple of the games with some lads from my halls. When the final arrived, early in the morning, instead of being at a pub and watching the game on the big screen, I was watching on my own in the common room. I was struggling and I was 'hibernating' again. I watched the final, a very rare sporting achievement for England, alone in the common room. I so much wanted to be apart if the celebrations but I couldn't face the crowds. It was the same watching England play in the 2002 Football World Cup. Most of the England's games were televised really early in the morning, but I so much wanted to be in the pubs, surrounded by the masses, singing and shouting and just enjoying the moment. Again earlier this year, England played in the European Football Championships. I'm a huge sports fan. I kept thinking to myself, as I sat in our front room watching the games that if England won the whole tournament, I'll become seriously depressed. I was worried how I would react if the whole country were out on the streets celebrating and I was hiding away because I didn't feel up to it. On the other, I am

English, and England and football has always been, in my lifetime, a no-win situation.

I am a social person by nature. I was very good as an Archery, Rifle Shooting and Fencing coach because I enjoyed what I did and I enjoyed spending time with the people I was teaching. I would love to feel part of a large group of friends again, knowing that I had people I could rely on and people who could also rely on me. I hate being known as a loner or somebody who has no friends. It hurts because it's a sad indictment of my life, of what I've achieved, or haven't achieved, over the years. I think being in a large social group and having friends would mean that I would stop my obsessive self-analysis. Because I feel under so much pressure to get back to the person I was, I critically analyse every mistake I make. I become analytic paralytic. This adds to the pressure and I end up crumbling again. To know friends are there to help you through these times would help. They'll make you laugh or cry, or perhaps be so honest with you that it hurts, but they'll get some kind of reaction out of you, and help you move on rather than dwelling on your mistakes.

I suppose I just want to feel accepted. I want to be able to say whatever is on my mind, and not care about the consequences or question what I've said. I want to be able to feel that what I say is as important as what anybody else says. I want to feel normal again. I'm tired of being someone who can be summed up by a mental term or by a particular anti-depressant. When I look back on my life, my most cherished memories have been with my big sister or when I was with a large group of friends. I was much younger, but I was much happier as well. In the past, my recent past, I have made some decent friends at work. People like me and I get on easily with others. This is another dream that's also close to becoming reality.

Something else that I would like to accomplish is to stop living my life through other people's hard work. When I am able to work, I work. I have proved it in the past and I have nothing to feel ashamed about. However, I would not like to admit to anybody that I live off benefits, or to be more precise, Incapacity Benefit. I get this because I produce a 'medical note', which is better known as a 'sick note'. I get these from my doctor and I absolutely hate having to ask for them. I hate the feeling that I'm being supported by millions of hard working people. I feel bitter and angry that I should have to live my life this way. I suppose my attitude and feelings towards this subject show that there is a spark of life still in me. I want to be earning my own way again. I want to feel that I've done the hard work and therefore I deserve to reap the rewards. The problem with living on benefits, apart from the fact you never have enough and you're always having to be careful with your money, is that nothing is ever yours. You don't really own it because you didn't really earn it.

It's another burden I would love to lift from shoulders because I feel cheap and lazy spending other peoples' money. I hate having to explain to the people at the benefits office that I find being out in public really difficult. I have to go and see the benefits staff because a lot of the time, my money is delayed and I have to trek down there to find out why. I don't want to be in that place. I want to hold my head up high like every other hard working person and not think about the social stigma of living on benefits. Sometime in the future, I will have to go for an assessment to see if I can continue to claim benefits. It is a series of questions, on a one-to-one basis. The questions range from how I find life, to whether or not I have a physical reason that I cannot work. To continue receiving benefits, you need to get a score of around fifteen points. Points are based on the severity of the case and the answers you give. I've always failed because I do not have a physical reason that I cannot work. I have a mental reason and that is deemed not serious enough. Being in the room and having these questions and the scrutiny of the person asking them is an horrible experience. I believe that people who decide who does and doesn't receive benefits think that I'm lying to them. This makes me feel totally bewildered, and somewhat angry.

I want earn my own money, hopefully doing something I enjoy and something that I'm good at. I want to go shopping and drinking with my girlfriend and my rowdy bunch of friends. I want the chains that leaden me with guilt to be cast away and never even considered again. I want to buy somebody a drink or a present and feel that it's my hard work that has paid for it and not a government cheque. I want my pride restored and I know my ambitions will play their part. It is hard to describe the stigma attached to somebody of my age relying on handouts. My father has worked all his life. He receives benefits because of an industrial accident. My mother, who spent her whole life bringing up three kids and working part-time and then full time, is waiting for an operation for complications with her spine. She and my father and millions like them have paid thousands in taxes and they deserve a damn site more than what they are getting. I have paid very little into the system and yet I continue to live of others, like my parents and millions of hard working people.

One of the biggest obstacles I have to overcome is the way in which I see the world. I think it is far too easy, and I feel, far too condescending to simply label me as the type of person who sees the glass half empty and not half full. I wish it were that simple. I know that it is the way I see things that leads me to so much trouble. I knew it when I was at University and I couldn't do anything to stop my decline. I become absolutely bombarded with negativity. When the thoughts and negative feelings arrive, the affect is like a tidal wave. There is a horrible, daunting familiarity, to my life. I "recover" from my depression enough to return to work, and then, between three and six months later, I end right back on benefits and back to feeling like I'm a lost and hopeless case. I rarely get angry with myself nowadays. Why can't I fend off these awful questions and damaging thoughts? I have tried. Then, I think of how much damage I cause myself if things go wrong. Whenever conviction or commitment is called for, I always assess how long it'll take me to recover, and then how long it'll be before things go wrong again. I hate to admit that. It is clearly wrong and I know that if I could have a more positive approach to life, then things might be better.

I am in the best possible hands because I am now talking with a Clinical Psychologist. I will be taught how to change the angle of my approach to my thoughts. I have been waiting for this chance for so long. I've talked to many counsellors, but they're not equipped to help me change my thought patterns. I look forward to speaking to my Clinical Psychologist because I desperately want stop destroying my own confidence. I know I have identified that it is the way I deal with the situation that has such a devastating affect on me. Instead of responding positively or thinking about how to deal with the situation, I am filled with loathing and self-doubt. The same questions come time and time again.

The possibilities and doors of opportunity that would open up for me are endless. I could and would take rejection and triumph in a balanced view. I'd love to enjoy the good times and not worry about when they are about to end. Ironically, once I realise that I am having or experiencing a 'good' moment, I tense up and think to myself that I should enjoy it to the maximum because it will be over soon. I despise thinking like that, but that's me, that's what defines me. I don't expect to live like Julie Andrews in the 'Sound of Music', singing and smiling my way through the trying and tedious times in life. I just want an equal share, an equal opportunity. I want to find some balance in my life.

To feel I can approach life in the same, or very similar attitude as most others would be incredible. I'm tired of feeling like a victim or fool who is powerless to control his own destiny. I keep saying to myself, almost like a mantra, just give me a chance, just one more chance to show the world what I have to offer. I think that I have so few good times in my life, that when they do occur I put too much pressure on myself to enjoy them to the full, and the good of the moment passes me by. It's a goal of mine that I can work towards because at the moment, I am doing my very best to get back on top, to feel that I can walk outside without feeling I don't belong or I have nowhere to go. I have a certain amount of faith in myself. It is that way because I have fallen on my face so many times after picking myself up again.

As I look to the future, all I have written about in this chapter can be described as top priority 'stuff'. They are all important to me. My immediate future is obviously the most important thing to consider. It's all very well making plans for the future, but if I don't get a grip on things in the short-term, then I won't have the faith to believe that there's a horizon for me. I am not going to go into a long, convoluted description of how my dreams always ending up hurting me. I want to focus on getting started with these ambitions for a future. I have started seeing a Clinical Psychologist and I have also amended my diet to an extent. I don't consider buying 'junk' food anymore. I run at least four times a week and the nights I don't run, I usually go for long walks. My aim is to enjoy my exercise and walking helps me to do this. I'm not quite a phoenix, but I am, slowly healing again. I don't want to think about all the times I've been in a similar situation, only to find myself back where I started.

There is a reason that I have been able to fight back. Oddly though, for the first time that I can recall, it has nothing to do with university. I don't think I will ever return there. I have been greatly helped by my sessions with my Psychologist; she is slowly chipping away at my constant stream of negativity. What has become my magnet, my attraction, is my writing. I have written many short stories and a few scripts. My strongest subjects at school, and then again at the numerous colleges I attended, was always English. I loved to write stories when I was younger. I was never too great on grammar or punctuation, but then again, I always got marked for the content of the story. I have a pretty creative imagination under all my woe and negativity. One of my most cherished memories in life is when a teacher in college read out my short story, 'Operation Dirty Betty'. Everybody laughed - which was good because it was supposed to be funny! I sat at the front of the class, glowing with pride, but typically me, in a very subdued manner. The reason I went to university was to learn as much as I could about all types of writing, and hopefully make some kind of career out of it. I have memories of sitting at a table in a busy café on the holiday centre, Mill Rythe, which means I was only about nineteen, writing all the words that I didn't understand from all the books I'd read. I did this because in the story I was writing at the time, I was going to swamp in big words that nobody had ever heard of. I told anybody who listen that I was writing a book.

Writing this story of my life and my struggle with depression is the beacon that pulls me through my present misery. I want to portray the endless days of 'nothingness' that I have seen. Even as I've been writing this, I have had some really bad days, but the one constant factor for the last few months is my dedication and commitment to finish this story. It is something that allows me to walk around feeling like I am a person who is going somewhere. It gives my life meaning and a purpose. Before this, before writing this account of my life, I was waking each day, full of regret and bitter recriminations. I couldn't get started in the morning. Rather, I would do what I always seemed to do, look back and mourn my failures. Those failures are still there, of course they are. Some of the memories that I've sifted through have affected me in extreme ways. I can laugh and enjoy some of the things I've done. My life hasn't always been the downhill slope that I sometimes think it is. On the other hand, I have walked away from some great opportunities in life, just the same as everybody else.

Writing this book has definitely helped me to put my life and my failures into some much needed perspective. I have been advised, over the years, by members of my own family and a few of my friends to write my feelings down on paper. I always agreed and told them I would think about. Years ago, I couldn't see myself doing anything like this. Yet, the only thing that I feel truly comfortable with is writing. Mainly the creative type, but writing anything. I have wanted to become a writer longer than I have had my obsession with going to university. I suppose that going to university and studying 'Media Writing' was like pursuing two dreams at once.

When I am relaxed and in the right 'mood' for writing. I have developed some really good ideas and strong characters. Yes, after a while I get the familiar questions about 'do I really think that anybody would want to read anything that I've written?'. That kills my creative flow, but at least I got some pleasure out of writing. I love reading and I adore the way a words on paper can become so meaningful and powerful. They can stop you and make you think. Words are so important. We live our lives speaking languages, but often loose the beauty of what is actually behind the words. When I am able to write, when I am relaxed enough to be able to concentrate, I forget about the person I am. It's as if I have entered a world where I know I am still me, but all the emotional baggage and stress is gone, buried or banished to the corner. Writing makes me feel like I have as much right to be on this planet as anybody else. I see talent within myself and it hurts that I have never been able to sustain it or make the most of it.

When Darin, my literary agent, suggested the idea of writing about my life, I was very noncommittal. I wasn't sure and my confidence didn't give me licence to believe that I could get anywhere near to becoming published. Writing my life story has been very therapeutic and cathartic. As well as my sessions with Nicola, my psychologist, I feel I have a better insight into how my mind works and possibly the areas in my life that I can identify and, in time, heal and correct - especially if I pass on this information to Nicola. I have worked damned hard on this account of my life. I have revisited times that I thought I had forgotten and some shadows in my past that I wished I would not have recalled. I have exposed my very soul to be analysed and pointed at. I know there are millions of other people who are suffering the same invisible torment as myself, and some much worse. I want my story to be heard because it is real, authentic and valid. Maybe, it will help others. I am not a moral crusade. I want to be published because I have put so much hard work in this. It will become my catalyst that will ignite my desire and drive for life. I want to experience the highs and lows of life, and react and deal with them like any other person. I want to feel proud and be able to face the person in the mirror with the comfort of knowing that I have achieved an ambition that is so vitally important to me.

Having my work published would mean so much to me. It would help to exorcise so many ghosts that have been haunting my mind for many years. It will mean that I have finally achieved something that I hold very dear to my heart. It will help to heal much of the hurt, and possibly bring attention and focus upon an illness that too few people understand. I want to feel proud of something that I've achieved, something which can help others as well.